U.S. MEDIA AND ELECTIƆ   ̅ FLUX

Paid, earned, and social media are all crucial element of modern electioneering, yet there is a scarcity of supplementary texts for campaigns and election courses that cover all types of media. Equally, media and politics courses cover election-related topics, yet there are few books that cover these subjects comprehensively.

This brief and accessible book bridges the gap by discussing media in the context of U.S. elections. David A. Jones divides the book into two parts, with the first analyzing the wide array of media outlets citizens use to inform themselves during elections. Jones covers traditional, mainstream news media and opinion/entertainment-based media, as well as new media outlets such as talk shows, blogs, and late-night comedy programs. The second half of the book assesses how campaigns and candidates have adapted to the changing media environment. These chapters focus on earned media strategies, paid media strategies, and social media strategies.

Written in a concise and accessible style, while including recent scholarly research, the book will appeal to students with its combination of academic rigor and readability. *U.S. Media and Elections in Flux* will be a useful supplementary textbook for courses on campaigns and elections, media and politics, and introductory American politics.

David A. Jones is Professor of Political Science at James Madison University.

"'Stay tuned.' That's the book's closing sentence, and one of the most prescient such sentences ever. David Jones has masterfully captured the dynamic and evolving role of the media in U.S. elections. The book is a must read for any citizen, journalist, politician, scholar, or student who seeks to understand the nature of contemporary election communication."

Thomas E. Patterson, *Harvard University*

"David Jones has written a lively book about the media in flux. He does a great job capturing all the extraordinary changes that have taken place in earned, paid, and social media. Students will gain a deep understanding of the shifting communications landscape."

Darrell West, *Brookings Institution*

"Jones offers an invaluable glimpse into contemporary political communication research. The content is at once complex and accessible, with current examples that will draw readers in and hold them tight. Amply documented, with invitations for deeper probing, *U.S. Media and Elections in Flux* provides the tools needed for a sophisticated exploration of political campaigns in an increasingly messy media environment."

Stephen Maynard Caliendo, *North Central College*

"This book takes a complicated, and ever-changing, area of American electoral politics and breaks it down in such a way that both the expert and novice have much to gain from reading it. I highly recommend it for courses in campaigns and elections, mass media and politics, and public opinion."

Jeffrey L. Bernstein, *Eastern Michigan University*

U.S. MEDIA AND ELECTIONS IN FLUX

Dynamics and Strategies

David A. Jones

Routledge
Taylor & Francis Group

NEW YORK AND LONDON

First published 2016
by Routledge
711 Third Avenue, New York, NY 10017

and by Routledge
2 Park Square, Milton Park, Abingdon, Oxon OX14 4RN

Routledge is an imprint of the Taylor & Francis Group, an informa business

British Library Cataloguing in Publication Data
A catalogue record for this book is available from the British Library

Library of Congress Cataloging in Publication Data
Names: Jones, David A. (David Adam), 1965-
Title: U.S. media and elections in flux : dynamics and strategies /
David A. Jones.
Other titles: United States media and elections in flux
Description: New York, NY : Routledge, 2016.
Identifiers: LCCN 2015035508 | ISBN 9781138777293 (hardback) |
ISBN 9781138777309 (pbk.) | ISBN 9781315772721 (ebook)
Subjects: LCSH: Mass media--Political aspects--United States. |
Communication in politics--United States. | Elections--United States. |
Political campaigns--United States.
Classification: LCC P95.82.U6 J67 2016 | DDC 324.7/30973--dc23
LC record available at http://lccn.loc.gov/2015035508

ISBN: 978-1-138-77729-3 (hbk)
ISBN: 978-1-138-77730-9 (pbk)
ISBN: 978-1-315-77272-1 (ebk)

Typeset in Bembo
by Taylor & Francis Books

Printed and bound in the United States of America by Publishers Graphics,
LLC on sustainably sourced paper.

For Wendy and Alex

CONTENTS

BOXES

INTRODUCTION

"Study: Major Shift in Media Landscape Occurs Every 6 Seconds," reads the headline in *The Onion*, the website that spoofs the news media. It's a joke, of course. But like all good satire, the story contains an element of truth. When it goes on to say that "the way information is transmitted and received in our culture is radically altered over 10 separate times in one minute," the only exaggeration may be the word "minute."[1]

The media landscape in the United States has shifted dramatically in the past few years, and the pace of change is breathtaking. These changes have altered the way Americans experience elections—the keystone of representative democracy. Despite these changes, however, what voters see, hear and read about elections remains the product of a push and pull between traditional news outlets and the candidates and campaigns they cover. Social media, talk shows and other forms of "new media" have shaken things up—fundamentally, in some ways—yet many voters still rely on television and newspapers to inform themselves, sometimes inadvertently. It is thus crucial to understand what conventional election news coverage looks like, how it gets produced, and the strategies and tactics campaigns employ to shape that coverage.

It is also important that a growing number of Americans supplement their election news diet with relatively novel alternative media outlets. Talk shows on cable television and radio attract relatively small, narrow audiences of like-minded people who seek out opinionated analysis of elections on a national and sometimes state level. Blogs and other internet sources aggregate news and opinion for even narrower audiences. Late-night comedy programs entertain and inform their audiences by mocking the candidates and the journalists who cover them. Meanwhile, with all these new choices available, many Americans opt out completely and do not vote.

Also changing are the ways in which people encounter election-related news, opinion and entertainment. Some people still read the morning paper or watch the evening news on television. But for a growing number of Americans, their first encounter with a story is when a friend shares a link on Facebook or a headline pops up on their Twitter feed. Others, especially older Americans, forward email messages to each other as a means of sharing content that traditional media outlets may ignore.

The changing media environment has important implications for campaign strategy. TV ads are no longer limited to television; now they are posted online and circulated by supporters. Opinion and entertainment-based media outlets give candidates more opportunities to reach voters more directly and informally. Social media platforms make the communication process more horizontal, empowering activists, volunteers and voters to provide and share a larger portion of information. Yet campaigns cannot completely bypass mainstream news outlets, much as many of them would like to. Journalists take their jobs very seriously. Elections thrive when voters are well-informed about the candidates and issues at stake, and it remains the responsibility of journalists to scrutinize the candidates' record, behavior and performance, among other things. Campaigns must—and do—work with the news media, and savvy campaigns manage the media in ways that account for the norms and needs of modern journalists. Campaigns also must continue to spend at least half of their campaign contributions on old-fashioned TV ads.

The purpose of this book is two-fold: (1) to survey the ever-changing media landscape in the context of elections in the United States, and (2) to assess how campaigns have adapted to these changes in terms of "earned media" and "paid media" strategies. Underlying the analysis are two general arguments:

1. Traditional news organizations remain the most important sources of election information for most Americans. Campaigns still expend a great deal of time and energy shaping how their candidates get covered in newspapers and on television. New opinion and entertainment-based media outlets depend on the basic reporting and news content provided by traditional media outlets, not the other way around.
2. Yet the top-down model of news providing is being replaced by a more horizontal process that gives citizens more control over the information they receive. A growing number of Americans get their election news "on demand" rather than "by appointment." It is easier for people to seek out media outlets that complement—rather than challenge—their existing opinions. And social networking outlets foster information sharing among rank-and-file voters, activists, volunteers, and the campaigns they support.

The book is split into five chapters. Chapters 1–2 examine the content providers that inform, entertain, affirm and even persuade voters during election season.

Chapter 1 focuses on traditional news media, particularly newspapers and televisions news programs. These outlets are commonly referred to as the mainstream media, abbreviated MSM. On what aspects of the elections do MSM focus? More importantly, why? In other words, what explains traditional media's tendency to focus less on the candidates' policy ideas and more on the "horse race"—who is ahead, who is behind, and the strategies and tactics the campaigns are employing to help them win? What explains the negative tone that characterizes so much of election news? When candidates make mistakes or get caught in a scandalous act, a media "feeding frenzy" usually ensues—days if not weeks of round-the-clock news coverage of the misdeed and what it means for the candidate's chances. Why do some blunders get more coverage than others? How do voters respond to these feeding frenzies?

This chapter will include a special section on what is perhaps the most compelling question surrounding news coverage of elections: Are traditional media biased toward Democratic candidates and the policies they espouse? In 2008, content analysis reveals that news coverage was much more generous toward Barack Obama than John McCain. How much of this was a product of "liberal bias," and how much of it stemmed from other media biases? In answering these questions, this chapter—along with subsequent ones—will go beyond conventional wisdom and speculation and dig deeply into the latest academic research on these subjects. In addition to describing patterns of traditional election news coverage, it will employ the research to offer explanations for these patterns. In other words, it will answer not only the "what?" questions, but it will also explore the "why?" and the "how?"

Chapter 2 turns to relatively new content providers. Many Americans now supplement their MSM diet with alternative outlets, especially during election season. Some of these outlets seek to entertain through political humor on late-night comedy such as *The Daily Show* on Comedy Central and *Saturday Night Live* on NBC. Young voters rely heavily on these sources for political information, raising questions about how informative they are and whether their parody shapes voters' impressions of the candidates. But this chapter is mostly concerned with opinion-based sources—talk shows on radio and television as well as blogs and other websites that filter election news through a partisan lens. Nationally syndicated talk radio has been an electoral force at least since the early 1990s. On cable television, Fox News and MSNBC provide elections news that may—or may not—carry a partisan tilt, but the bread-and-butter of these networks are the highly charged talk shows aired during prime time. On the internet, voters can get their election news filtered through partisan news aggregators such as *The Huffington Post* and *The Drudge Report*. Opinion-based media outlets attract small but loyal audiences of mostly like-minded people. Their growth gives Americans more opportunities to selectively expose themselves to news and opinion that is compatible with their existing worldview. How many Americans actually take advantage of these enhanced opportunities for selective exposure? For the people who do tune in, how impactful are these outlets in general and during elections in particular, especially in light of the like-minded nature of their audiences? To what extent do they push their already partisan audiences further to the extremes?

By the end of Chapter 2, readers will have gained an understanding of the modern media environment, both in terms of its dramatic transformation as well as its more static qualities. Part II of the book shifts to what all of this means for campaign strategy. In addition to academic research, Chapters 3–5 will draw upon insights provided by campaign professionals. In Chapter 3, the subject is how campaigns and candidates manage the news—what campaign professionals call earned media strategies. One approach has been to bypass traditional news organizations as much as possible and instead reach voters through friendly opinion-based media and entertainment outlets. But as Chapter 1 reminds us, traditional media outlets cannot be ignored. Readers will be introduced to a wide range of approaches ranging from standard press conferences, photo-ops and press releases to candidate appearances on talk shows. The chapter includes a box on "Damage Control," which reviews the practices that campaigns employ when their candidate gets caught on camera making a controversial statement or is embroiled in a scandal. In addition, readers will see that campaigns attempt to shape media coverage by: (1) managing expectations about how well candidates might do in debates and other highly mediated events and (2) controlling journalists' direct access to the candidate.

Whereas earned media is sometimes called "free media," campaigns spend most of the money they raise on what is aptly called "paid media," primarily television advertising. Compared with the chaos of earned media, campaigns have much more control over all aspects of this form of communication with voters. But is it money well spent? What impact does campaign advertising have on the attitudes and behavior of voters? Chapter 4 explores this question by synthesizing the latest academic research on the subject with examples from recent national, state and local elections. It also examines trends in the content, format and placement of campaign advertising. Voters say they loathe negative ads, but campaign professionals are convinced that they work. Does academic research support this assumption? In 2012, both presidential campaigns spent millions on television advertising, nearly all of it negative, but the Obama team used targeted ad buys made in advance to get more for their money while the Romney campaign paid top dollar for prime-time slots. Did these efficiencies help Obama win the election? Results are mixed, as we will see in Chapter 4.

Campaigns are turning to social media platforms such as Facebook and Twitter to compensate for some of the pitfalls of conventional earned and paid media. On social media, ads and other communication may be microtargeted to individual voters whose political views and behavior have been revealed by their online activity. Rather than pay tens of thousands of dollars to run a 30-second spot on television, a campaign may post it—or longer versions of it—on YouTube and encourage its supporters to share with their Facebook friends and Twitter followers. If the video is controversial or unusually clever, it might get covered in the news media or discussed on a talk show. As a result, the video can be viewed by thousands of voters without the campaign buying much if any airtime. Chapter 5 examines this and other ways that campaigns are using social media to bypass conventional outlets and reach voters online, either directly or through their online networks. Readers will see social media help campaigns enlist supporters to raise money, persuade undecided voters, and mobilize other likely supporters to the polls. In addition to anecdotal evidence from recent elections, it will draw upon research examining the effects of social media on information flow, perceptions of candidates and voter mobilization.

Elections remain largely mediated experiences. In other words, much of what Americans experience during the course of an election campaign happens through various media, new and old. This book explores what modern mediated elections look and sound like and how the campaigns themselves attempt to shape these elemental communication processes. Campaigns have struggled to keep up with the constantly changing media environment, as have the media outlets themselves. The conclusion summarizes these transformations, then turns to a few emerging trends and events that suggest additional shake-ups. By the time readers finish this book, the electoral implications of these phenomena may be readily apparent.

Note

1 "Study: Major Shift in Media Landscape Occurs Every 6 Seconds." *The Onion*, November 28, 2013. http://www.theonion.com/articles/study-major-shift-in-media-landscape-occurs-every,34690/?ref=auto

1

THE NEWS MEDIA

By most measures, the news media are in deep trouble. Newspaper circulation has declined steadily for two decades, as have audience ratings for television news. Both are losing eyes and ears to talk shows and other opinion-based outlets, which are attracting small but growing audiences of highly engaged citizens. Many younger voters are getting their "news" from late-night comedy and other entertainment-oriented programming (Chapter 2). A swiftly growing number of Americans are getting their election news via Facebook, Twitter and other online social media platforms (Chapter 5). News organizations have adapted by massively escalating their online presence, allowing them to preserve and sometimes expand their audiences. But online advertising has fallen short for news organizations: there is plenty of it, but it earns nowhere near the revenue of conventional print ads and TV spots.

All of this means that campaigns can ignore the news media, right? Not so fast. Many voters still watch and read "the news" and turn to traditional media outlets to provide it. According to the 2013 report on "The State of the News Media" by Pew Research Center's Project for Excellence in Journalism, newspaper circulation may have stabilized after many years of steady decline. In 2012, about 22 million people reported watching the evening news on either ABC, CBS or NBC—down only slightly from 2008. Local television viewership dropped more sharply during that period, but nearly half of respondents reported that they still watch their local news regularly (Pew Research Center's Project for Excellence in Journalism 2013a). Most Americans over the age of 50 remain regular viewers of television news (Pew 2013a) and—as any campaign professional will tell you—these people vote regularly. Overall, although the report paints a disturbing portrait of steady decline, its findings remind us that traditional news media are still crucial sources of information during elections.

Indeed, for media coverage of major election-related events, live television is still where mass audiences gather. In 2012, for example, election night news coverage by the network and cable news networks attracted 66.8 million viewers during prime time, only slightly less than the record audience of 71.5 million people who watched televised news coverage of Barack Obama's historic victory in 2008 (Stelter 2012a). The first debate between Obama and Mitt Romney was watched by 67.2 million people on television at home—the largest audience for a first debate since the 1980 matchup between Ronald Reagan and then-President Jimmy Carter (Stelter 2012b).

It is true that the ground has shifted. As we will see in subsequent chapters, social media platforms and other online media outlets provide a relatively cost-effective means of bypassing the news media and communicating with voters directly. Yet without traditional news organizations, there wouldn't be much news to opine about on a talk show or blog, spoof on late-night comedy, tweet on Twitter, or share on Facebook. Journalists, whether they work for a traditional news outlet or an online startup, provide nearly all the original reporting that makes up the news. For this reason alone, maintaining a working relationship with professional reporters remains the most important part of a campaign's "earned media" strategy. It thus makes sense to develop a comprehensive understanding of how journalists cover elections, why they cover elections in these ways, and the impact of modern election news coverage on how voters think and behave.

Who Are the News Media?

This chapter focuses on the *news media*. These are media outlets that are primarily concerned with providing the news—that is, information about current events—as reported by professional journalists. Traditionally the news media are also called the "press," a holdover from when most journalists worked for newspapers. Today they are commonly referred to as the mainstream media (sometimes abbreviated as the MSM). On the print side, examples include daily newspapers, the most prominent of which serve both a local and national audience—e.g., *The New York Times* and *Washington Post*—or are purely national in scope—e.g., *The Wall Street Journal* and *USA Today*. The Associated Press and other wire services supply national and international news stories to local newspapers and websites around the country. On television, examples of the news media include local television news broadcasts, the nightly network news, and the news operations of 24-hour cable news channels. All of these news media outlets have a significant presence online in the form of websites, Facebook pages, and Twitter feeds. Indeed, these outlets now reach most of their readers and viewers online.

News media outlets are staffed by journalists—reporters, editors, producers, etc.—who work together to produce "stories" about current events. Journalists are professionally trained in their craft, and that training includes an emphasis on professional norms. The most important norm is to cover the news *objectively*—that is, in an even-handed, neutral, fair and balanced or non-partisan fashion. Objectivity emerged as a journalistic norm in the 20th century, and it did so for a variety of reasons. This was the century of the "mass media," when audiences were huge and politically diverse. By covering political events in a neutral manner, media outlets could present the news without offending large portions of their audience. After World War II, the Federal Communications Commission implemented the Fairness Doctrine, which required television and radio broadcasters to cover controversial information in a balanced manner—a regulation that remained in place until the late 1980s. Meanwhile, journalism was shifting from a blue-collar profession to one that required a college degree, and the journalism schools ("J-schools") that attracted many would-be reporters, editors and producers reinforced objectivity and other professional norms (West 2001).

Today, it seems hopelessly naïve to think anyone—even a trained reporter—could report the news objectively. Even so, it remains a goal of most professional journalists. This professional norm sets journalists apart from talk show hosts and bloggers, who are primarily concerned with expressing their opinions or interpreting the news in a one-sided, sometimes inflammatory fashion.

For all their faults, journalists are also keen to provide good "newsworthy" stories that are fair, accurate and important—or, "buzzworthy," to use the contemporary term. Sometimes they are driven by selfish motivations: they strive for professional prestige by authoring stories that lead the news broadcast or appear on the front page; stories that go viral on social media; stories that win journalism awards. Yet these selfish motivations are not always incompatible with the needs of a democratic society. Democracies need their media to, at minimum, inform citizens about public affairs and scrutinize the actions of the powerful. Modern journalists are motivated to produce rigorously reported news stories that "make a difference." Their role models are more likely to be Bob Woodward and Carl Bernstein, the *Washington Post* reporters who broke the Watergate story, not Fox News talk show host Bill O'Reilly or MSNBC's Rachel Maddow.

It is also true, however, that most journalists in the United States work for profit-seeking news organizations that are part of a larger corporation. The largest newspaper chain, Gannett, owns *USA Today* and a variety of local newspapers, as well as 43 television stations across the country. Comcast isn't just a cable and internet provider—it also owns NBC, MSNBC, and 24 local television stations. Rupert Murdoch's News Corporation has an enormous global reach—in the U.S., News Corp. holdings include Fox News on cable television, the Fox broadcast network, and *The Wall Street Journal* and the *New York Post* newspapers. CBS Corporation owns not only the broadcast network (including CBS News) but also 29 local television stations and 130 CBS radio affiliates. ABC is owned by Disney. In 2012, Warren Buffett's Berkshire Hathaway Company bought 23 daily newspapers from the troubled Media General Company chain. Other news organizations are privately owned, including *The Washington Post*, purchased in 2013 by Amazon founder Jeff Bezos, the *Philadelphia Inquirer, Milwaukee Journal-Sentinel*, the Minneapolis *Star Tribune*, and the *Columbus Dispatch* in Ohio.

The bottom line: nearly all news organizations in the U.S. are businesses, and businesses strive to make profits. That means generating sufficient revenue while controlling costs. And since most news organizations are part of publicly traded corporations, it isn't enough to merely make a profit—they are pressured to enhance the company's ability to *increase* profits over time.

The problem is, two-thirds of the news revenue comes from advertising (Pew 2013a), and advertising revenue has dropped sharply since the 1990s, especially for newspapers. Newspapers have been devastated by the nearly complete loss of classified advertising to Craigslist and other online sources. They also have been hard hit by declines in industries that had spent heavily on print advertising for much of the 20th century: department stores and auto dealers. Newspapers have expanded their readership online, but online advertising revenues are nowhere near enough to compensate. According to one study, for every $1 gained in online advertising revenue, newspapers have lost $7 in print advertising (Pew 2013b). Meanwhile, television news audiences are aging, which means news programs are less attractive to advertisers aiming to reach viewers between the ages of 25 and 54—widely seen as the "sweet spot" for consumer spending. Once a source of huge profits for media corporations, advertising revenue for television news is now flat (Pew 2013a).

Faced with a grim revenue situation, media outlets have cut costs by scaling back their news operations. The number of full-time editorial jobs at newspapers plummeted from 56,400 in 2001 to 36,700 in 2014, according to the American Society of Newspaper Editors (2014). The *Star-Ledger*, New Jersey's largest newspaper, cut 25 percent of its newsroom staff in April 2014. The New Orleans *Times Picayune* cut half of its newsroom staff in 2012. Even *The New York Times* has eliminated newsroom positions. The *Washington Post* editorial staff has been cut dramatically.

Naturally, these cutbacks have had a negative impact on news coverage of elections. Presidential campaigns still get intense, round-the-clock scrutiny. But local news media now lack the reporting resources to thoroughly cover state, local and Congressional elections. Stretched thin across multiple beats, many local newspaper and television reporters have neither the time nor the incentives to develop a particular expertise. Instead, much of the shrinking news hole for election news is filled by stories supplied by wire services, especially the Associated Press, which naturally are less equipped to provide local news. The 2002 race for governor of California was the focus of less than one percent of local news broadcast in the month of October (Iyengar 2011). According to one study, 92 percent of local news broadcasts in the month before the 2004 elections contained *no stories at all* about campaigns for the U.S. House and state and local offices. Based on content analysis of local news broadcasts in 11 media markets, this study reported that TV stations ran five times more paid advertisements by House and Senate candidates than news stories about their races (Kaplan, Goldstein and Hale 2005). In short, both the quantity and quality of election news have taken a hit.

Some of these developments are old news. The U.S. media environment has been highly commercialized since the advent of the penny press in the 19th century. Business pressures have always placed constraints on good journalism. But now more than ever, news organizations compete with each other—as well as providers of more entertaining fare—for the eyes and ears of the American public. The resulting content is a mixed bag: plenty of high-quality information for news junkies with the means and motivation to pay for it, but increasingly thin, superficial, sensational and fundamentally flawed fare for less discerning citizens.

Patterns of Elections News Coverage

What does all of this mean for the content of election news? On what aspects of elections do the news media focus? Ideally, the news media will provide information about candidates' issue positions and policy platforms, relevant background characteristics, and past performance. What is the reality? *How* do the news media cover elections?

Interpretation and Analysis

One long-term trend that has shaped election news coverage has been the decades-long shift toward more interpretive journalism (West 2001). The tendency accelerated in the 1970s, by which time the shortcomings of conventional objective reporting had become apparent. While traditional objective news aimed to be fair and balanced, critics charged that it lacked the context voters needed to make sense out of the factual information being presented. Objectivity was partly blamed for political failures that could have been prevented had the media been more aggressive and less balanced. In their coverage of the Vietnam War, the news media failed to challenge the Pentagon's rosy assessments until it was too late. Had the news media stretched the limits of objectivity and raised tough questions about Richard Nixon's character and personality, he would have lost the 1968 election, and the Watergate scandal would have never happened. During the 1988 election, the media acquiesced to the George H.W. Bush campaign's focus on crime as a campaign issue at a time when Republicans were seen as the anti-crime party. These perceived failures led journalists to question the practice of passively reporting what the candidates say without challenging the merits of what they are saying. According to political scientist Shanto Iyengar (2011):

> after the 1988 campaign, leading reporters argued that recycling candidates' message of the day was an inappropriate form of campaign journalism because it made reporters captive to the agenda of campaign consultants. To protect their autonomy, reporters turned to a more analytic form of news coverage

that centered on interpretations and analysis of the candidates' actions ... The campaign correspondent was now a solo author of the news, whose own analysis was more newsworthy than what the candidates had to say.

(p. 72)

By the 1990s, journalists had shifted from merely *describing* campaigns to fully *analyzing* them. A key aspect of reporting became "reading between the lines" to unearth the true meaning of what candidates were saying and doing. Today, if a candidate makes a false claim about an opponent, journalists are apt to not only challenge the information, but also attempt to explain *why* the guilty campaign resorted to spreading falsehoods ("Behind in the polls, Candidate A stepped up his negative attacks on Candidate B ..." a story might report). In other words, rather than merely report what a candidate said, the news media will analyze *why* the candidate said it. This strategic framing of election news invites audiences to conclude that politicians are more concerned with winning elections than debating the merits of various policy solutions. Election news analysis rarely allows for the possibility that a politician is sincerely motivated to make good policy.

Sometimes the media become less analytical at the wrong time. When the situation calls for more analytical scrutiny of the substance of candidate statements and potential policy outcomes, the media cautiously err on the side of objectivity—even when one side is clearly wrong. Critics calls this "false balance" or "false equivalence"; Democratic consultant James Carville calls it "Neil Armstrong Syndrome":

Candidate A says the moon is a cold hard rock covered with craters. Candidate B says the moon is a huge chunk of green cheese with bites taken out of it. Local newspaper covers the exchange with a headline stating "Candidates Trade Charges about the Makeup of Moon"—but no reporter calls Neil Armstrong to ask him what he actually found when he landed there in July 1969. Rather Candidate A's evidence (scientific data, newspaper articles) will be cited but often given equal weight with Candidate B's evidence (whatever the campaign can find on somebody else's letterhead).

(Dunn 1994: 117)

Reporters "frequently defend themselves by saying their job is to report the news, not play the referee in the fight, and that citizens can make up their own minds about who is right and who is wrong" (Dunn 1994: 117). Yet as we will see, the media seem perfectly willing to play the referee in deciding who is winning the fight. There is a lot of analysis, but not about the things that matter.

More Negativity

A related trend is that election news has become increasingly negative in tone. Republicans are convinced that the media are biased against them in favor of

Democratic candidates and the issues they represent, and sometimes that appears to be the case (see Box 1.1 below). In reality, however, the media tend to be biased against politicians of all political stripes—a "preference for the negative" rather than a consistent liberal bias (Patterson 2002: 374). When John F. Kennedy ran for president against Richard Nixon in 1960, positive media references to the candidates outnumbered negative references by a three-to-one margin. By 1992, there were far more negative than positive references, a tendency that has continued for subsequent presidential elections. In 2000, for example, nightly network news coverage of George W. Bush was 63 percent negative and only 37 percent positive; Al Gore's coverage was similarly negative (Patterson 2002).

BOX 1.1 LIBERAL MEDIA?

Among many conservative Republicans, it is a truism that the news media are biased in favor of Democrats. Are they correct? Surveys indicate that journalists lean to the left on most issues and vote accordingly (Lichter and Rothman 1986; Wilhoit and Weaver 1991). And some studies indicate that mainstream news coverage leans to the left, at least under certain circumstances (Groseclose and Milyo 2005; Schiffer 2006). In one study, all of the major national news outlets are shown to have a liberal bias except two: the *Fox News' Special Report* and the *Washington Times*, both of which are widely viewed as conservative media anyway (Groseclose and Milyo 2005). Similarly, Adam Schiffer (2006) found evidence of relatively favorable election news coverage of Democratic candidates in local newspapers, which is consistent with research on media coverage of a U.S. Senate race in Minnesota (Druckman and Parkin 2005). One set of experiments revealed that left-of-center journalists made decisions in ways that reflected their political leanings (Patterson and Donsbach 1996).

Other perspectives cast doubt on the liberal bias charges. In the 2012 election, Obama fared no better than Romney (Sides and Vavreck 2013). Although reporters may lean to the left, other forces—the value placed on objectivity and other norms of journalism, the influence of editors and other supervisors—largely prevent their views from seeping into news coverage (Gans 1979; Zaller 1996). Rather than root for a particular candidate, the news media are more likely to root for a "good story," which may explain why Romney's coverage improved when the 2012 race tightened (Sides and Vavreck 2013). Rich and Weaver (1998) showed that conservative think tanks get slightly more coverage than identifiably liberal ones. And several other studies found little or no evidence of ideological bias either way (D'Allessio and Allen 2000; Niven 1999; Page 1996). Some critics argue that conservative critics have it backwards—that the media's corporate ownership and other factors contribute to a climate that is more favorable to conservative causes than liberal ones (Alterman 2003). In his classic account of reporters covering the 1972 campaign, Crouse (1973) turned on its head the assumption that liberal reporters favor Democratic candidates:

> It is an unwritten law of current political journalism that conservative Republican Presidential candidates usually receive gentler treatment from the press than do liberal Democrats. Since most reporters are moderate or liberal Democrats themselves, they try to offset their natural biases by going out of their way to be fair to conservatives ... If a reporter has been trained in the traditional, "objective" school of journalism, this ideological and social closeness to the candidate and his staff makes him feel guilty; he begins to compensate; the more he likes and agrees with the candidate *personally*, the harder he judges him *professionally*.
>
> *(pp. 355–356)*

It could be that media bias is in the eye of the beholder. Research on the "hostile media phenomenon" consistently shows that partisans on the left and right tend to view information reported in the mass media as unfavorable to their own point of view (see, for example, Vallone, Ross and Lepper 1985; Gunther and Schmitt 2004; Schmitt, Gunther and Liebhart 2004; Perloff 1989). This may explain why liberals are sometimes just as disgruntled with the media as conservatives (Jones 2004): both groups of partisans view mainstream news organization as biased against their viewpoints.

Yet conservatives have offered the most sustained complaints about media bias. Even if the evidence is mixed, there is no doubt that conservative Republicans—both at the mass and elite level—*perceive* the media as being uniquely hostile to their candidates (Jones 2004). That perception explains in part the success of Fox News as an enclave for conservative viewers fed up with the mainstream media.

Why so negative? Political scientist Thomas Patterson blames post-Vietnam acrimony between journalists and politicians as well as the rise of an interpretive journalism, which accentuates candidates' failures and downplays their successes (Patterson 1994). But a recent study of 2012 campaign coverage reminds us that sources often drive a story, and most sources for campaign news are motivated to say negative things about their opponents (Pew 2013a). In other words, it was the sources who were negative, not the journalists who quoted them. It is also true that equal-opportunity negativity is compatible with journalistic norms. "Although norms of American journalism dissuade reporters from taking sides in a partisan debate, there is no rule that says they can't bash both sides" (Patterson 2013: 16).

Negative news also relates to the news media's interest in *conflict*. This interest should not be surprising. By nature, an election is a conflict between two or more candidates, each usually representing one of the two major parties. That conflict is real: the policy and ideological differences between the two parties has widened over the past two decades, and campaign rhetoric reflects those differences. To some extent, election news is simply reporting that conflict rather than creating it. But it is also true that the news media will sometimes exaggerate the conflict-related aspects of the campaign. Negative campaign commercials get more media attention than positive ads (Ridout and Smith 2008). Debates are framed as "battles" and get more press when candidates make them look more like "brawls" than if they are more polite to each other. Candidates learn that one way to make news is to shake up their usual stump speech—which reporters have heard dozens of times and is therefore no longer news—and launch a new attack on their opponent. Conflict sells, and news organizations know it. So do campaign strategists.

Perhaps negative news is simply more compelling—to journalists, of course, but also audiences. Americans complain about how depressing the news is, but are they not more likely to read a story about a candidate's dumb mistake than an analysis of their position on entitlement reform? Critics call it "attack journalism," but journalists say they are simply giving their audiences what they want.

Shrinking Sound Bite

Another manifestation of a more assertive media is what critics call the "shrinking sound bite." Election stories often feature candidate sound bites—that is, a block of uninterrupted talking by the candidate, usually an excerpt from a speech, a press event, or an interview. Until the 1980s, election stories tended to feature lengthy quotes from the candidates; in 1968, for example, the average sound bite on the nightly network news was about 43 seconds. By 1988, the average sound bite had shrunk to nine seconds (Hallin 1992), and it has hovered around that number ever since (Farnsworth and Lichter 2011). A similar pattern has emerged for newspapers (Patterson 1994). Instead of quoting the candidates, election stories turn to partisan sources and pundits, who offer their own commentary. The most prominent voices are now the journalists themselves. During the 2008 election, for example, 68 percent of on-air speaking time on the nightly network news was taken by journalists—either the anchor or correspondent—compared with only 23 percent by the candidates (Farnsworth and Lichter 2011).

It is possible that journalists' sound bites are beginning to shrink. In 2012, only 27 percent of the "statements in the media about the character and records of Barack Obama and Mitt Romney" came from journalists—nearly half of what it was in 2000. Why the decrease? Not a less aggressive media; instead, the researchers blamed the need for resource-strapped news organizations to rely on their sources for analysis (Pew 2013a).

Overall, journalists themselves figure much more prominently in campaign news stories than they did during the era of objective news. They no longer merely report what candidates say and do—they analyze the *why* and the *how*. Their analysis tends to carry a negative tone, often ascribing cynical motivations for candidates' behavior. In addition, their analysis gets more air time than the remarks of the candidates themselves. These tendencies raise additional questions. What exactly are journalists analyzing? What aspects of the election get more attention than others?

Newsworthiness

Journalists and the companies they work for share at least one goal: the production of *newsworthy* stories that attract audiences—especially stories that get widely shared on social media. Among journalists, there is quite a bit of debate about what constitutes a newsworthy story. But most would agree that the following elements should be considered:

Novelty: The word "news" says it all. News should be fresh and new; otherwise it is "old news" or "yesterday's news." If a television news operation or news website can report live "breaking news," all the better.

Drama: Elections are inherently dramatic because they pit one side against the other in a conflict with a clear resolution. Needless to say, tight races are more newsworthy than elections easily won by incumbents coasting to victory.

Prominence: The actions of politicians, celebrities and other elites warrant more attention than ordinary people. Similarly, incumbent candidates often get more news coverage than their challengers, especially challengers who are far behind in the race. Usually, the higher the office, the more the coverage by national media and even local media.

Human interest: Some subjects are naturally compelling because of the personalities, backgrounds, and personal histories of the individuals involved in the story. Sometimes candidates themselves are a "good story" because of what they represent—Barack Obama in 2008, for example, who went on to become the country's first African-American president. Donald Trump also is an irresistible story.

These priorities partly explain why campaign news so often focuses on who is ahead and who is behind, the private lives of candidates, and the mistakes they make.

Horse Race Journalism

Presumably voters would benefit from thorough coverage of the candidates' issue positions, their qualifications and record, along with relevant biographical information. But the news does not provide much information about these subjects. Most election news stories focus on the "horse race," "game" or strategic aspects of the campaign—that is, which candidate is ahead, which candidate is behind, and what strategies the campaigns are employing to win the election (Patterson 1994). Many of these stories report the results of opinion polls. Others might focus on how much money the campaigns have raised—i.e., who is winning (or losing) the fundraising race. Others stories synthesize the analysis of experts—sometimes called "pundits" or "talking heads"—who assess the state of the race and what each side needs to improve their chance of winning. As these headlines illustrate, the focus of horse race stories is on strategy and tactics, not policy platforms and candidate qualifications:

"Eric Cantor Brings in Big Bucks for Primary Challenge," *Roll Call*, May 30, 2014

"Marco Rubio, Rick Perry Run TV Ads in Iowa," *Sunshine State News*, May 29, 2014

"McAuliffe Leads Cuccinelli in Virginia Governor's Race," *Washington Post*, September 23, 2013

"Corzine Points a Spotlight at His Rival's Waistline," *The New York Times*, October 7, 2009

"Dean Holds Strong Lead over Kerry in N.H. Poll," *Boston Globe*, September 7, 2003

The preponderance of horse race news rises and falls depending on the election, but it always tops the list of most widespread story frames. According to a study of the nightly network news on CBS, ABC and NBC, 60 percent of presidential election news coverage in 2008 focused on the horse race (Farnsworth and Lichter 2011). Horse race coverage is even more prominent during primary elections. That is because primary contests pit members of the same party against each other, which mutes the policy-related differences between the candidates, making issue-based coverage even less compelling than it is during a general election between Democrats and Republicans. During the 2012 primaries, nearly two-thirds of news coverage was framed in terms of the horse race (Pew 2013a).

It should not surprise us that horse race stories are more prominent than stories about the candidates' policy platform, background and record. For starters, horse race stories benefit from the "novelty" factor described earlier. Polls go up and down, as do fundraising numbers, and campaigns are constantly making new strategic decisions to enhance their chances. By contrast, policy positions do not change much unless a crisis emerges that requires a response from the candidates (as was the case in 2008, when Obama and McCain had to flesh out their reactions to the economic crisis, then in its early stages). Because they tend to remain unchanged, issues rarely constitute "the news." A candidate who alters an issue position in the middle of a campaign risks being labeled a flip-flopping opportunist—a policy-focused story that is best avoided. Otherwise news organizations tend to limit their issue-based reporting to a one-time or occasional summary of the candidates' platforms.

Horse race stories also benefit from being relatively dramatic, especially if the election is close (in 2012, news outlets were accused of exaggerating the closeness of the race in an effort to attract audience). They are entertaining and easy to digest, and audiences seem to like them. In one study, researchers gave subjects a CD containing a large number of election news stories about three weeks before the 2000 election; the stories focusing on the horse race proved to be the most popular—much more so than the issue-based stories on the CD (Iyengar, Norpath and Hahn 2004). Horse race stories also lend themselves to more straightforward, objective coverage in part because they draw upon concrete reports such as poll results and campaign finance documents. By contrast, policy stories—especially those involving interpretation and analysis—invite the reporter to take a side.

The news media's natural horse race orientation has other effects besides more stories focused on campaign strategy and poll results. It also shapes where news organizations allocate precious resources. Especially now, media outlets cannot afford to assign a reporter to cover every race in their market. Even national news organizations are reluctant to assign reporters except to candidates who establish themselves as viable contenders. Who decides which candidates are viable? The news media, who look to poll results and fundraising totals—i.e., the horse race—as indicators for what constitutes a good story worth covering. A tight race is a good story. So is an underdog candidate who is beating expectations and posing a serious threat to an established incumbent. Hopeless and longshot candidates can be interesting and therefore worth a "human interest" story or two, but not sustained coverage.

Sometimes news outlets are misled by the horse race. David Brat was a classic "hopeless candidate" when he challenged Majority Leader Eric Cantor for the Republican nomination in the race for Virginia's 7th Congressional District. Cantor had a wide lead in the polls and in fundraising, and national and regional media gave scant coverage to the race. But a reporter for the *Chesterfield Observer*, a weekly newsletter that serves the Richmond suburbs, wrote several stories hinting that Cantor was in trouble. The reporter's shoe-leather reporting turned out to be more accurate than the traditional horse race indicators: Brat won by 11 points (Carr 2014).

Private Lives

Election news tends to be negative in part because of the media's interest in politicians' personal failures. Stories about candidates' private lives, their personal flaws, and their personality quirks are appealing to journalists and audience members alike. After all, such coverage meets the "human interest" criterion of newsworthiness. Who can resist a story about Mitt Romney leashing the family dog to the roof of a car? How about Bill Clinton's extramarital affairs? Candidates are human beings, each with their own personalities. They tend to be ambitious and smart, but—like all human beings—they make mistakes and sometimes engage in questionable behavior. All of this is relevant: journalists point out that past and present private actions can predict candidates' decision-making once in office. So when New York gubernatorial candidate (and then-Congressman) Anthony Weiner texted sexually explicit photos to women both before and during his marriage, his behavior was not merely revolting—it showed poor judgment, especially for someone seeking higher office. It thus should not surprise us that candidates' personal scandals, odd behavior and personality quirks are popular fodder for election news coverage.

For traditional news organizations, such topics were off limits until a few decades ago. Reporters looked the other way when President Kennedy recklessly engaged in extramarital affairs partly because his actions were seen as irrelevant to the job of President. That changed with the Watergate scandal. Running for reelection in 1972, President Richard Nixon approved a series of "dirty tricks" against his political foes, culminating in the burglary of the Democratic National Committee's D.C. headquarters located in the Watergate office. *The Washington Post* investigation of the Watergate break-in exposed not only the White House effort to cover up its role in the break-in, but also troubling aspects of Nixon's personality: his bizarre paranoia; his desire to not only defeat but discredit his opponents; his racist and anti-Semitic views.

For many journalists, a lesson of Watergate was that "character matters"—that personality flaws can lead to public misdeeds (West 2001). For candidates, this eventually meant that their private lives would be scrutinized by the news media. U.S. Senator Gary Hart learned this the hard way when he ran for the 1988 Democratic Presidential nomination. Hart had been besieged by rumors that he had been engaged in extramarital affairs. Following an investigation, the *Miami Herald* published a story that led with the following: "Gary Hart, the Democratic presidential candidate who has dismissed allegations of womanizing, spent Friday night and most of Saturday in his Capitol Hill town house with a young woman who flew from Miami and met him." At a press conference three days later, *Washington Post* reporter Paul Taylor asked Hart, "Have you ever committed adultery?" Taylor was pilloried for asking what was then seen as a tawdry question, as was the *Herald* for breaking the story, but the episode signaled a shift in media oversight of politicians' personal lives. Hart had engaged in reckless behavior despite intense media scrutiny—in fact, he seemed to flaunt it, at one point challenging the media to "Follow me around. I don't care. I'm serious. If anybody wants to put a tail on me, go ahead. They'll be very bored." How would he behave as President, journalists reasoned? Whereas Watergate justified the close investigation of candidates' personality, the Hart story legitimized digging even deeper into the private lives of politicians.

Still, traditional news organizations sometimes struggle to determine whether such information is worth reporting. In 1996, for example, the *Washington Post* decided against publishing the results of an investigation of allegations that Republican presidential candidate Bob Dole had had an affair while married to his first wife in the late 1960s. The editors killed the story not because the information was untrue, but because the affair seemed irrelevant to Dole's qualifications as President and it had happened so long ago (Downie and Kaiser 2003). In today's media environment, however, the *Post*'s restraint would be irrelevant. While *Post* editors fact-check and wring their hands about relevance, online outlets would simply post a story based on rumors alone. Indeed, even though the *Post* ended their investigation, the *National Enquirer*—a tabloid newspaper—broke the story in October before the election.

Gaffes

Questions about newsworthiness also surround news coverage of gaffes. A gaffe is a verbal miscue or other mistake made by a politician that results in negative media coverage. Sometimes gaffes are controversial or offensive remarks, such as when Senate candidate Todd Aiken implied in an interview with a local TV news reporter that there was such a thing as "legitimate rape." Others are seemingly accidental verbal slip-ups—for example, when an apparently confused President Gerald Ford claimed during a televised presidential debate that there was "no Soviet domination of Eastern Europe"—in 1976, at the height of the Cold War. Still others are non-verbal; Michael Dukakis's disastrous tank photo-op comes to mind. If the gaffe resonates, what follows is a media "feeding frenzy"—that is, "the press coverage attending any political event or circumstance where a critical mass of journalists leap to cover the same embarrassing or scandalous subject and pursue it intensely, often excessively, and sometimes uncontrollably" (Sabato 1993: 6). Talk show hosts and late-night comedy shows pile on, mocking the candidate, sometimes for days on end.

Candidates are human beings, and human beings make mistakes. What kinds of gaffes warrant sustained news coverage? Gaffes seem to catch fire when they crystalize the existing narrative about a candidate. Just as a scandal can expose a character flaw, a gaffe can expose a defining characteristic of the candidate. To reverberate with the media and their audiences, a gaffe must underscore the stereotype associated with the candidate, not challenge it. For example:

- At a closed-door fundraising during the 2012 presidential campaign, Republican candidate Mitt Romney essentially wrote off 47 of Americans when he said:

  > There are 47 percent of the people who will vote for the president no matter what … who are dependent upon government, who believe that they are victims, who believe the government has a responsibility to care for them, who believe that they are entitled to health care, to food, to

housing, to you-name-it … And the government should give it to them. And they will vote for this president no matter what … These are people who pay no income tax … [M]y job is not to worry about those people. I'll never convince them they should take personal responsibility and care for their lives.

Romney's remarks struck a chord partly because he was speaking candidly, unaware that he was being filmed. A bartender secretly videotaped the speech using his smartphone, then leaked it to Mother Jones magazine, which posted it online. But the gaffe also reverberated because it played into the existing narrative that Romney was an out-of-touch plutocrat. To his critics, this was the "real Romney" caught on tape speaking his mind.

- Also at a closed-door fundraiser, this one toward the end of the 2008 Democratic primaries, Barack Obama was caught on audio tape fretting over voters who "get bitter … and … cling to guns or religion, or antipathy toward people who aren't like them, or anti-immigrant sentiment, or, you know, anti-trade sentiment [as] a way to explain their frustrations." To his opponents, these remarks epitomized Obama's holier-than-thou tendency to patronize people who disagree with him. This candidate narrative reemerged four years later when Obama used a speech to explain his position that wealthy people should pay higher taxes: "If you've got a business—you didn't build that," he said, pointing out that government-funded schools, infrastructure also contributed to their success. To critics in the media and elsewhere, the remark crystalized Obama's anti-business image.
- During his 1998 campaign for president, Democrat Michael Dukakis rein-forced his detached, dispassionate image during the second presidential debate when asked whether he would support the death penalty if his wife had been raped and murdered. Rather than challenge the CNN reporter for asking an offensive question, he calmly explained his opposition to the death penalty, then changed the subject to illegal drug policy. Dukakis did not mention his wife.
- Bob Dole was 73 years old when he ran for President in 1996, 23 years older than his opponent, President Bill Clinton. Voters were reminded of Dole's age several times during the campaign, but most dramatically when he fell off the stage of a campaign event in Chico, California. Dole was uninjured, but television clips of the incident and Dole's grimaced expression and feeble appearance highlighted the age gap.
- Running for the 2012 Republican presidential nomination, Texas Governor Rick Perry had promised to cut spending in part by eliminating three cabinet departments. But during one of the Republican debates, he couldn't remember the name of the third department: "The third agency of government I would do away with—the education, the uh, the commerce and let's see. I can't the third one. I can't. Sorry. Oops." Perry had underperformed in

previous debates, magnifying his image as an unprepared lightweight, and the "oops" gaffe solidified this impression.

- George Allen's "Macaca" moment: Republican George Allen was supposed to coast to reelection in the Senate against Democrat Jim Webb in 2006. But the race was tighter than expected, and at a campaign rally three months before election, Allen singled out a Webb campaign volunteer of Indian descent—the only non-white person at the event—and twice referred to him as "Macaca." The volunteer was there as a "tracker," which means it was his job to follow Allen around and film him, hoping to catch a gaffe on tape. That is exactly what happened. The Webb campaign pointed out that "Macaca" was a racial slur in some contexts, the tracker's video went viral, and a media feeding frenzy ensued. The incident also triggered additional reporting of racially insensitive actions by Allen in the past, and Allen eventually lost the race.

How costly are gaffes and the media coverage of them? We can only speculate on whether the "47 percent" remark, the "oops" stumble, the "Macaca" slur, and other stumbles cost their candidates the election. Whatever damage Obama's "bitter" and "You didn't build that" comments caused, he won anyway. But we do know that gaffe stories are irresistible to the reporters who are covering the candidate. They have heard the same stump speech over and over again, and they are desperate for something new to cover. When Fox News President Roger Ailes was still a Republican strategist, he came up with an "orchestra pit theory" of journalism to describe the appeal:

> It goes like this: a presidential candidate can give the most important speech of his career on a topic that is the number one priority of the voters[,] but if he falls into the orchestra pit on his way off the stage, all the networks and newspapers will report the stumble and ignore the speech.
>
> *(Sparrow 1999: 34)*

News Media Effects

Does election news coverage shape voters' impressions of the candidates? Campaigners think it can—otherwise they wouldn't try so hard to influence media coverage of their candidate. One scholar observed that "[w]hen campaigners are asked about the importance of the media, most respond with disbelief that the question need be asked and an inability to convey adequately the perceived importance" (Arterton 1984: 8). Yet academic research offers mixed evidence on the breadth and depth of news "media effects." On one hand, voters rarely change their minds in direct response to media messages. On the other hand, the media can exert subtle influences on the thinking and decision-making of voters, and these effects can have short and long-term consequences. Although the news media seldom *persuade* voters to support one candidate over the other (nor are they usually interested in doing so), they can shape issue priorities (the *agenda-setting* effect), evaluation criteria (the *priming* effect) and the way in which people think about issues and candidates (the *framing* effect).

Early research suggested that media messages had only negligible impact on the attitudes and behavior of audiences. In part that is because researchers were looking for evidence of direct persuasion. Finding none, scholars concluded that the media had "minimal consequences" on candidate preferences, which was attributable to voters' propensity to filter out information that ran counter to their existing predispositions. Rather than persuade people to change their minds, the media merely *reinforced* existing beliefs. The absence of measurable effects also stemmed from the relatively balanced content of election news, especially on television. As this chapter has shown, traditional news coverage of major races rarely favors one side over the other on a consistent basis—indeed, all candidates tend to suffer from more negative than positive news. The tone of a candidate's coverage tends to go up and down depending on a variety of factors, including her/his relative position in the polls. By election day, both major candidates had their good weeks and (mostly) bad weeks in the news media. Voters have used a variety of outlets to watch, read and hear both positive and negative about both candidates, but mostly negative, minimizing the likelihood that one candidate would fare better than other due to news coverage.

What happens when elections news is clearly one-sided? Although Obama and Romney were treated about the same in 2012, McCain fared far worse than Obama in 2008. Yet McCain lost the 2008 election for a host of reasons, the most important of which stemmed from a poor economy. Sometimes, though, one-sided coverage can be consequential, especially for non-presidential elections during which voters are less saturated with information and messages. In the 2000 race for one of the Minnesota seats in the U.S. Senate, news coverage by the Minneapolis *Star Tribune* was slanted toward Democrat Mark Dayton over Republican Rod Grams, the incumbent. This slant seemed to have a direct impact on voters' evaluations of Dayton and may have influenced their vote choice (Druckman and Parkin 2005). In a study of newspaper coverage of Senate races contested between 1988 and 1992, voters showed a preference for candidates that had been endorsed by their local newspaper, in part because endorsed candidates benefited from news coverage slanted in their favor (Kahn and Kenney 2002).

Other media effects are less direct, yet no less important. One is called the *agenda-setting* effect. Under this theory, the media play a key role in determining which issues matter the most to voters simply because they focus on some issues and minimize others. In other words, the media "may not be successful most of the time telling people what to think, but it is stunningly successful in telling its readers what to think *about*" (Cohen 1963: 13). Under the corresponding *priming* effect, these issue priorities become, in turn, the criteria by which voters evaluate political leaders, including candidates running for office. The priming effect hurt

John McCain in 2008, when the media focused on the economic crisis—an issue that would hurt any Republican candidate at the time because its party controlled the White House. Similarly, the priming effect disadvantaged incumbent George H.W. Bush in 1992, when stories about the sluggish economy replaced triumphant coverage of the Gulf War that had dominated the news a year earlier. When Jimmy Carter ran for reelection in 1980, he may have been a victim of the priming effect when, during the closing days of the campaign, the media turned its attention toward negotiations over releasing American hostages in Iran—an issue that clearly favored his opponent Ronald Reagan (Iyengar 2011). Priming effects can be dramatic during primary elections, when the absence of issue-based conflict prompts the media to focus even more attention on the horse race. Primary voters are therefore primed to evaluate the nominees in terms of the likelihood that they will win.

A related effect is called *framing*. Framing describes the process by which the media organize, structure, and apply themes to stories, and the corresponding impact of this manner of presentation on audiences. By changing the way in which a story is presented, the media can shape voters' perceptions of the candidates, issues and events covered in the story. Usually, the news media frame issues *episodically*—that is, they focus on specific events and individual cases. Less common is the use of a *thematic* frame, which provides a broader perspective by incorporating historical factors, policy-making dynamics, and collective outcomes. When the media frame a problem episodically, voters tend to blame the problem on the individuals depicted in the story. Thematic frames tend to encourage voters to attribute the problem to broader societal factors and blame government officials and institutions for failing to address them (Iyengar 1991). Accordingly, if the media were to employ the thematic frame more often, perhaps voters would demand more creative policy solutions from candidates running for office.

Conclusion

Journalists take their jobs very seriously. They strive to write accurate, important stories that people will read, watch and/or share with others. But most journalists work for corporations that need to sell advertising, and that need favors certain stories over others. Journalists may not be driven by the profit motive of their employer, but they are affected by it. And these pressures are greater than ever. As a result, the news media spend less time covering issues and more time on such topics as who is ahead and who is behind, campaign strategy, and the mistakes candidates make. These stories are relatively easy to produce and audiences seem to enjoy them.

These tendencies are frustrating for politicians running for office and the staffers who support them. Candidates want to talk about what they will do if they win the election, and their staffers push them to be clear and consistent, even at the risk of sounding repetitive. Reporters need candidates to do or say something new, even if that means falling off the stage. After winning the 1976 presidential election, Jimmy Carter observed:

> It's strange that you can go through your campaign for president, and you have a basic theme that you express in a 15- or 20-minute standard speech that you give over and over; and the traveling press—sometimes exceeding over 100 people—will never report that speech to the public. The peripheral aspects become the headlines, but the basic essence of what you stand for and what you hope to accomplish is never reported.
>
> *(Patterson 1994: 147)*

Carter overstates his case: most serious news outlets will report on the candidates' policy platform. But they might do so only once unless something changes. Otherwise it's old news.

References

Alterman, Eric. 2003. *What Liberal Media? The Truth about Bias and the News*. New York: Basic Books.

American Society of Newspaper Editors. 2014. "2014 Census." http://asne.org/content.asp?pl=121&sl=15&contentid=387.

Arterton, F. Christopher. 1984. *Media Politics: The News Strategies of Presidential Campaigns*. New York: Free Press.

Carr, David. 2014. "Eric Cantor's Defeat Exposed a Beltway Journalism Blind Spot." *The New York Times*, June 14. http://www.nytimes.com/2014/06/16/business/media/eric-cantors-defeat-exposed-a-beltway-journalism-blind-spot.html?_r=0.

Cohen, Bernard C. 1963. *The Press and Foreign Policy*. Princeton, NJ: Princeton University Press.

Crouse, Timothy. 1973. *The Boys on the Bus*. New York: Ballantine.

D'Alessio, Dave, and Mike Allen. 2000. "Media Bias in Presidential Elections: A Meta-Analysis." *Journal of Communication* (Autumn): 133–156.

Dalton, Russell J., Paul A. Beck and Robert Huckfeldt. 1998. "Partisan Cues and the Media: Information Flows in the 1992 Presidential Election." *American Political Science Review* 92(1): 111–126.

Downie, Leonard, Jr., and Robert G. Kaiser. 2003. *The News about the News: American Journalism in Peril*. New York: Knopf.

Druckman, James, and Michael Parkin. 2005. "The Impact of Media Bias: How Editorial Slant Affects Voters." *Journal of Politics* 67(4): 1030–1049.

Dunn, Anita. 1994. "The Best Campaign Wins: Local Press Coverage of Nonpresidential Races." *Campaigns and Elections American Style*, ed. James A. Thurber and Candice J. Nelson. Boulder, CO: Westview.

Farnsworth, Stephen J., and S. Robert Lichter. 2011. *The Nightly News Nightmare: Media Coverage of U.S. Presidential Elections, 1988–2008*, 3rd edition. Lanham, MD: Rowman & Littlefield.

Gans, Herbert. 1979. *Deciding What's News*. New York: Vintage.

Groseclose, Tim, and Jeffrey Milyo. 2005. "A Measure of Media Bias." *Quarterly Journal of Economics* 120(4): 1191–1237.

Gunther, Albert C., and Kathleen Schmitt. 2004. "Mapping Boundaries of the Hostile Media Phenomenon." *Journal of Communication* (March): 55–70.

Hallin, Daniel C. 1992. "Sound Bite News: Television Coverage of Elections, 1968–1988." *Journal of Communication* 42(2): 5–24.

Iyengar, Shanto. 1991. *Is Anyone Responsible?: How Television Frames Political Issues*. Chicago: University of Chicago Press.

Iyengar, Shanto. 2011. *Media Politics: A Citizen's Guide*, 2nd edition. New York: Norton.

Iyengar, Shanto, Helmut Norpath and Kyu S. Hahn. 2004. "Consumer Demand for Election News: The Horserace Sells." *Journal of Politics* 66(1): 157–175.

Jones, David A. 2004. "Why Americans Don't Trust the Media: A Preliminary Analysis." *Harvard International Journal of Press/Politics* 9(2): 60–75.

Kahn, Kim Fridkin, and Patrick J. Kenney. 2002. "The Slant of the News: How Editorial Endorsements Influence Campaign Coverage and Citizens' Views of Candidates." *American Political Science Review* 96(2): 381–394.

Kaplan, Martin, Ken Goldstein, and Matthew Hale. 2005. "Local News Coverage of the 2004 Campaign: An Analysis of Nightly Broadcasts in 11 Markets." A report by the Lear Center Local News Archive, a project of the USC Annenberg School and the University of Wisconsin.

Lichter, S. Robert, and Stuart Rothman. 1986. *The Media Elite: America's New Powerbrokers*. Bethesda, MD: Adler and Adler.

Niven, David. 1999. "Partisan Bias in the Media? A New Test." *Social Science Quarterly* 80(4): 847–858.

Page, Benjamin. 1996. *Who Deliberates? Mass Media in Modern Democracy*. Chicago: University of Chicago Press.

Patterson, Thomas E. 1994. *Out of Order*. New York: Vintage.

Patterson, Thomas E. 2002. "The Vanishing Voter: Why Are the Voting Booths So Empty?" *National Civic Review* 91(4): 367–377.

Patterson, Thomas E. 2013. *Informing the News: The Need for Knowledge-Based Journalism*. New York: Vintage.

Patterson, Thomas, and Wolfgang Donsbach. 1996. "News Decisions: Journalists as Partisan Actors." *Political Communication* 13: 455–468.

Perloff, Richard M. 1989. "Ego-Involvement and the Third Person Effect of Televised News Coverage." *Communication Research* 16: 1910–1926.

Pew Research Center's Project for Excellence in Journalism. 2013a. "The State of the News Media 2013: An Annual Report on American Journalism." http://stateofthemedia.org/.

Pew Research Center's Project for Excellence in Journalism. 2013b. "Newspapers Turning Ideas into Dollars: Four Revenue Success Stories." http://www.journalism.org/2013/02/11/newspapers-turning-ideas-dollars/.

Rich, Andrew, and R. Kent Weaver. 1998. "Advocates and Analysts: Think Tanks and the Politicization of Expertise." In *Interest Group Politics*, 5th edition, ed. Allan Cigler and Burdett Loomis. Washington, DC: Congressional Quarterly Press.

Ridout, Travis N., and Glen R. Smith. 2008. "Free Advertising and How the Media Amplify Campaign Messages." *Political Research Quarterly* 61(4): 598–608.

Sabato, Larry J. 1993. *Feeding Frenzy: How Attack Journalism Has Transformed American Politics*. New York: Basic.

Schiffer, Adam J. 2006. "Assessing Partisan Bias in Political News: The Case(s) of Local Senate Election Coverage." *Political Communication* 23(1): 23–39.

Schmitt, Kathleen M., Albert C. Gunther, and Janice L. Liebhart. 2004. "Why Partisans See the Media as Biased." *Communication Research* 31(6): 623–641.

Sides, John, and Lynn Vavreck. 2013. *The Gamble: Choice and Chance in the 2012 Election.* Princeton, NJ: Princeton University Press.

Sparrow, Bartholomew H. 1999. *Uncertain Guardians: The News Media as a Political Institution.* Baltimore, MD: Johns Hopkins University Press.

Stelter, Brian. 2012a. "TV Ratings for Election Night Approached 2008 Record." *The New York Times*, Nov. 7. http://www.nytimes.com/2012/11/08/us/politics/tv-ratings-for-election-night-approach-2008-record.html?_r=0.

Stelter, Brian. 2012b. "Presidential Debate Drew More Than 70 Million Viewers." *The New York Times*, Oct. 4. http://mediadecoder.blogs.nytimes.com/2012/10/04/presidential-debate-drew-more-than-70-million-viewers/.

Vallone, Robert P., Lee Ross, and Mark R. Lepper. 1985. "The Hostile Media Phenomenon: Biased Perceptions and Perceptions of Media Bias in Coverage of the Beirut Massacre." *Journal of Personality and Social Psychology* 49(2): 577–585.

West, Darrell M. 2001. *The Rise and Fall of the Media Establishment.* New York: St. Martin's.

Wilhoit, G. Cleveland, and David H. Weaver. 1991. *The American Journalist*, 2nd edition. Bloomington, IN: Indiana University Press.

Zaller, John. 1996. "The Myth of Massive Media Impact Revived: New Support for a Discredited Idea." In *Political Persuasion and Attitude Change*, ed. Diana C. Mutz, Paul M. Sniderman, and Richard A. Brody. Ann Arbor, MI: University of Michigan Press.

2

NEW OPTIONS

What about new media outlets? In the previous chapter, we analyzed the state of "old media"—or, the news media, especially newspapers and television. We saw that although the news media are not well, they certainly are alive and remain vital during elections. Yet many Americans, especially younger ones, are gravitating toward new opinion-based and entertainment-oriented media outlets, online and on television. Some fall under the category of social media such as Facebook and Twitter, which—because they are better understood as *communication platforms* rather than singular sources of information—will be analyzed separately in Chapter 5.

This chapter will focus on the relatively new political media outlets that have emerged in what political scientist Markus Prior calls the "high-choice" media environment. As we will see, the expansion of cable news triggered not only the growth of mainstream cable news covered in the previous chapter, but also more opinionated talk and news programming. Opinion-based media outlets also flourish online in the form of blogs and highly partisan news aggregators. At the same time, late-night comedy has become an increasingly important source of political information, highlighting the thin line between news and entertainment.

More Choice

Americans now face a dizzying array of choices about where to get their information during elections. Some outlets are first-rate sources; others are less reliable. Some are highly partisan and opinionated; others are more even-handed. For many Americans, one common choice is to avoid election news altogether, which is more easily accomplished today (Prior 2007). All of these changes have important implications for voters, election results, traditional media and campaign strategy.

The changes are a boon to political junkies. Anyone with access to an internet-connected computer or device can pay to read election coverage from elite news outlets such as *The New York Times* and *The Wall Street Journal*. Highly engaged citizens also may turn to *Politico, Vox, FiveThirtyEight* and other online news providers that are devoted to politics and therefore serve as key information sources of election-related content. For more opinionated news and talk, citizens may turn on cable television for MSNBC or Fox News, tune in to Rush Limbaugh on the radio, or go online for blogs such as the *Huffington Post* and the *Drudge Report*.

For these highly engaged regular voters, how much better is today's media environment? Before the internet and cable television, media options were relatively limited. Local newspapers were fat with advertising and news stories, but quality varied outside of large cities. Broadcast television aired about 30 minutes of local news and another 30 minutes of national news, but much of the "news hole" was filled with reports on the weather, sports, and crime, as well as advertising. News coverage also tended to be pretty fair and balanced, rarely favoring candidates from one party over the other. News magazines combined depth and breadth, but they were distributed only once a week. Radio had declined as a major source of news (National Public Radio did not gain steam until the 1990s). Highly engaged citizens may have read their favorite newsmagazine over the course of a week and read their local paper and watched the evening news every day. But that was about all they had. And the content of the news was pretty tame—perhaps too centrist for engaged partisans who craved more commentary and analysis.

Today, traditional news outlets are just some of the options. For highly engaged citizens with high-speed internet access, the sky is the limit. They may now supplement their traditional news diet with an array of new media outlets: opinionated talk shows on television and radio; blogs and specialized news aggregators online; and political comedy on late-night TV and online. They may get their news online from previously out-of-reach elite sources such as *The New York Times, The Wall Street Journal*, and the BBC. It is a good time to be a news junkie.

What about the average citizen? It turns out that less engaged citizens may have been better informed when they had fewer choices. Before the internet and cable, the news was difficult to avoid. For lengthy periods several times a day— early in the morning, during the dinner hour, and late at night—local affiliates for all three major broadcast networks aired news programs and little else. A viewer who turned on the television between 6:00pm and 7:00pm ET might have only three programming options: the CBS Evening News, NBC Nightly News or ABC News. As a result, at least some news—including election news—was being consumed by a wider spectrum of citizens, even those who would have preferred to watch more entertaining programs. In today's high-choice media environment, people have plenty of other options on television and online—any time of the day—and many choose to avoid the news completely. Those who opt for entertainment over news miss out on the information to which, in the old "low-choice" media environment, they would have exposed themselves merely as a by-product of watching television. Because they now lack the information they need to evaluate candidates and issues, many of these citizens no longer vote at all. Meanwhile, news junkies are better informed and more engaged than ever. They tend to be highly partisan. And, as always, they vote (Prior 2007).

More Opinion

Many of the newer media options center on the expression of political opinion. Talk shows on the radio and cable television provide one-sided commentary that attracts small but devoted audiences. Blogs attract like-minded readers online, many of them seeking a digest of news and commentary that cater to their existing views. Even traditional news has become more opinionated.

Talk Shows

In terms of talk shows, radio led the way in the 1990s. Although call-in talk shows had existed for decades, radio programs tended to be local and low-tech. But with the advent of satellite technology, nationally syndicated radio programs could be transmitted live and with high-quality audio across the country. The cost of telecommunication dropped sharply in the 1980s, enabling radio programs to set up toll-free numbers so that listeners could call in and join the discussion. In 1987, the Federal Communication Commission dismantled the Fairness Doctrine, which had required that broadcasters include contrasting views when controversial issues were discussed on the air. Talk radio programs were no longer obligated to present a fair and balanced debate and could now be one-sided and highly partisan. By the mid-1990s, nationally syndicated political talk shows hosted by flamboyant personalities were mainstays of primetime radio programming.

Rush Limbaugh dominated talk radio for about 20 years starting in the early 1990s. For three hours every weekday afternoon, Limbaugh reaches a national audience of millions of followers; at his peak in the 1990s, it was estimated that he averaged 20 million listeners each week. His format became a template for the medium: a five to ten-minute monologue followed by questions from callers, most of them fellow-conservatives. Many of his callers referred to themselves as "dittoheads" as a means of expressing their agreement with what Limbaugh was saying on the air. Limbaugh spent much of his airtime lambasting liberal activists ("feminazi's" and "environmentalist wackos"), Democratic elected officials, and progressive political ideas and policies. He also scrutinized fellow Republicans, assessing their fealty to free-market principles. But his favorite target was the mainstream media, which he considers hopelessly biased in favor of liberals and against conservatives.

Fox News and MSNBC

Limbaugh's success demonstrated that conservative opinion-based programming could attract a large national audience. Today, talk radio continues to be dominated by conservative programs, with Mark Levin, Sean Hannity and Glenn Beck joining Limbaugh as top-rated shows. But the most dramatic development in conservative media has been the popularity of Fox News on cable television. In 1996, Republican operative Roger Ailes launched Fox News to serve "an under-served market in news"—a 24-hour cable news network for conservatives who were discontented with the so-called "liberal media" (Auletta 2003: 61). Like CNN, Fox News reports news throughout the day with full-hour news programs in the mornings and early evenings. But two of its prime-time slots are reserved for talk shows hosted by charismatic conservative personalities Bill O'Reilly and talk radio host Sean Hannity. Beck was lured from CNN and given his own show until he left the network in 2011. Another popular show was hosted by Mike Huckabee, candidate for the Republican presidential nomination in 2008. Huckabee left the network in 2015 to explore a possible presidential bid.

MSNBC eventually followed Fox's lead, but mostly on the left end of the political spectrum. The cable network was launched in 1996 as a joint effort by NBC and Microsoft to combine television news and online forces. Ten years later, it languished in third place behind CNN and Fox. That changed when the network began airing talk shows during prime time hosted by charismatic hosts, mostly on the left. Leading the way was Keith Olbermann, followed by Rachel Maddow, a talk radio host who was given the precious 9:00pm/ET spot, and whose show was an instant success. By 2010, the network had surpassed CNN in primetime and overall ratings in part by establishing itself as the liberal counterpart to Fox News. Its recent ratings struggles have led to some second-guessing about MSNBC's shift to the left, but its image as the liberal Fox News will be difficult to shake.

There is nothing inherently wrong with political opinions being expressed on talk shows. That is their purpose. But does opinion belong on news programs? Journalists are schooled and socialized in the norms of objectivity, balance and fairness. News organizations are expected to present information without partisan bias. They may fail (see Chapter 1), but they are expected to try.

Fox and MSNBC have been criticized for no longer trying to be objective. Fox News' motto is "Fair and Balanced," but content analysis reveals that its news programming is anything but (Groseclose and Milyo 2005; Jamieson and Cappella 2010). Initially, MSNBC's relationship with NBC News kept its news reporting in check. But by 2008, its news programming was under attack for being overtly supportive of Barack Obama over Hillary Clinton during the Democratic primaries, then over Republican John McCain during the general election. It did not help that the network's election coverage was anchored not only by journalist David Gregory, but also Chris Matthews and Olbermann, both of whom hosted left-leaning talk shows on the network. During the primaries,

Matthews famously admitted that he "felt this thrill going up my leg" when he heard Obama speak.

Both networks seemed true to form during the 2012 election. Between August 27 and October 21, 71 percent of MSNBC news stories about Romney were negative while only three percent were positive. On Fox, 46 percent of news stories on Obama were negative and only six percent positive (Pew Research Center 2012)

Drudge Report, Huffington Post and Other Online Outlets

Online, Americans can get relatively objective news from the websites of traditional news organizations (see Chapter 1), online outlets such as *Politico*, as well as home pages for Google, Yahoo and MSN. But for more opinionated content, they may turn to political websites and blogs that lean to the left or right. Conservative blogs include *Hot Air* and *Red State*; on the left, *Daily Kos* and *Talking Points Memo*. But the most popular outlets in this category are partisan news and opinion "aggregators" such as the *Drudge Report* and *Huffington Post*.

The *Drudge Report* has changed little since Matt Drudge launched the website in 1997. *Drudge* is remarkable for its simplicity and no-frills appearance. The main page consists mainly of a banner headline that links to the featured story, followed by three columns of secondary headlines—each in courier, typewriter-like font—with a few photos and ads haphazardly sprinkled in.

As with other news aggregators, nearly all of the stories are produced by mainstream news organizations. Drudge and his staff do very little reporting and produce very little original content. Exceptions include situations where Drudge hears about a story under production by a mainstream news outlet, then he breaks the story before its provider does by posting a two to three-paragraph preview. This happened in 1997 when *Newsweek* hesitated before publishing the results of its investigation of President Bill Clinton's relationship with intern Monica Lewinsky. While *Newsweek* sat on the story, *Drudge* posted a brief summary under the headline, "Newsweek Kills Story on White House Intern."

Aside from scooping other news providers, *Drudge* also serves as a media gatekeeper, picking and choosing stories that will interest his mostly conservative audience. During election season, that might include highlighting a story that provides damaging information about Democratic candidates. In 2012, for example, *Drudge* and other conservative media outlets (including Hannity on Fox News) hyped what they promised would be a bombshell video of "Obama's other race speech." The speech was made at Hampton University by then-Senator Obama in 2007, and the video captured Obama paying tribute to his controversial pastor, Rev. Jeremiah Wright. The story fizzled when it became apparent that the video had been available on YouTube since 2008, and that several news outlets (including Fox News) had covered the speech when it happened. Drudge was accused of being an overt promoter of Mitt Romney's candidacy, even during the Republican primaries. On election night, *Drudge*'s banner headline implied that Romney was ahead until late in the evening, when he begrudgingly announced Obama's victory with the headline, "Divided States of America."

Like *Drudge*, the *Huffington Post* aggregates news and opinion for a partisan audience, but with content and readers that lean to the left. It also is headed by a charismatic personality, columnist and activist Ariana Huffington. Also like *Drudge*, *HuffPo* relies heavily on stories provided by mainstream news outlets. Similarly, headlines are written to entice its partisan readers—although they are often hyperlinked to traditional news stories that are often tamer than the headline implies. With both websites, although content tends to support their respective political parties, they will occasionally challenge fellow partisans, as *HuffPo* did during the 2012 election when Obama stumbled during his first debate with Romney.

Compared with *Drudge*, however, *Huffington Post* also relies on a variety of regular contributors and bloggers. It has been much more aggressive in diversifying its content beyond politics to include extensive coverage of entertainment, celebrities, technology and business. Moreover, its design is much sleeker, and it attracts an even larger audience than does *Drudge*.

The success of *Drudge* and *Huffington Post* has inspired a host of other edgy online outlets featuring political content. The website *BuzzFeed* is best known for viral cat videos and entertaining "listicles"—"29 Things Every Foreign Student in Sweden Has Experienced," for example—but it also boasts a serious news staff that includes Pulitzer Prize winner Mark Schoofs. In 2011, *BuzzFeed* hired Ben Smith of *Politico* to serve as Editor-in-Chief. It now produces election news with headlines like "This is How Jeb Bush Plans to Reach Out to Latino Voters" and "These Are the States That Spent the Most Money on the 2014 Elections." The website Mashable lured an assistant manager editor away from *New York Times* to become its chief content officer. The *Washington Post* lost popular online columnist Ezra Klein to Vox, a website that specializes in serious analytical journalism (Mitchell 2014).

These new sites are designed for sharing via social media, much more so than direct viewing by users visiting the website on their own. Their election news items appear on Twitter and Facebook newsfeeds, inviting people to click on enticing stories. Some of those items go viral. According to Smith, *BuzzFeed* is more about "being part of the conversation" on social media than building a loyal audience for its website (Mitchell, Jurkowitz and Olmstead 2014). As we will see in Chapter 5, campaigns are employing social media strategies to shape those online conversations in ways aimed at helping their candidates. Whether election-related items compete with "The 40 Greatest Dog GIFs of all Time" will be a challenge for content providers and campaign strategists alike.

Clearly Americans have many new choices when informing themselves during elections. More and more of these choices are opinionated, either by design (talk show) or more subtly (cable news). So what? Opinionated news is not without precedent. Until the Civil War, news outlets were closely associated with the political parties. When the "penny press" first delivered newspapers to mass audiences, sensational tabloid-style stories dominated the front pages. It wasn't until the Progressive Era of the early 20th century that objectivity and other professional norms of modern journalism began to take shape. Newspapers—and later television—embraced objectivity in large part to avoid offending members of their audience and key advertisers (Schudson 1978; West 2001).

But by the middle of the 20th century, the limitations of objectivity and other journalistic norms were already becoming apparent. The existence of these norms may partly explain a number of media shortcomings and failures: the tendency of new organizations to rely on official sources of information; the failure to challenge Senator Joseph McCarthy and other crackpots; and the media's susceptibility to government deception (Cunningham 2003). For a variety of reasons, public trust in the media had plummeted by the end of the 20th century (West 2001). Americans had lost faith in the media's ability to report the news responsibly.

Even so, Americans still depend almost entirely on the media for exposure to political views unlike their own. And a case could be made that "exposure to conflicting views" is perhaps "the sine qua non" of "the kind of political dialogue needed to maintain a democratic citizenry" (Mutz and Martin 2001: 97). When individuals hear and read about opinions unlike their own, they learn to appreciate the perspectives of others; gain an appreciation for their own position; consider changing their mind; and grant legitimacy even when they disagree with the outcome. As sources of information about dissimilar views, media outlets are superior to interpersonal networks involving face-to-face communication. With the latter, diversity is hindered by the trend toward residential balkanization—with Republicans more likely to live next door to fellow Republicans; ditto for Democrats—and the corresponding tendency of people to seek out individuals like themselves (Huckfeldt et al. 1995). All of this results in "a disappointing tendency toward homogeneity." Media outlets are, by contrast, "hotbeds of diversity, not because the media are doing such an exemplary job pursuing diversity, but because individuals are doing such a poor one" (Mutz and Martin 2001: 110). Hence a potential problem with a more partisan media environment: if more and more news organizations orient themselves toward narrower, like-minded news audiences, their capacity for exposing people to diverse viewpoints would be diminished.

Theoretically, it is now easier for people to limit themselves to information sources with which they agree, and thereby isolate themselves from alternative perspectives. Conservatives can limit themselves to talk radio and Fox News. Democrats can rely on the *Huffington Post* and Rachel Maddow. Do they?

Partisan selective exposure. Today's media environment makes it easier for voters to engage in what social scientists call "partisan selective exposure." That is when individuals gravitate toward media outlets that are compatible with their existing beliefs and avoid oppositional sources (Stroud 2011). How widespread is partisan selective exposure? To what extent are Americans limiting their media diet to sources that lean in their direction?

Selective exposure may be less widespread than some fear. On one hand, survey evidence suggests that many partisans have migrated toward news sources that are perceived to be friendly to their beliefs. By 2004, for example, liberals were more likely to report watching *The Daily Show* and CNN and less likely to report tuning in to Fox News and *The O'Reilly Factor* (Coe et al. 2008). Similar patterns have been observed in experimental research. In one study, highly knowledgeable citizens favored news sources that coincided with their partisan beliefs, especially if they perceived the mainstream media to be biased (Stroud 2011). In an experiment that observed subjects' online news gathering, Republican subjects were much more likely to link to a story that was accompanied by a Fox News logo than if the story's logo was either from NPR, CNN or the BBC (Iyengar and Hahn 2009). A similar study of the 2000 election found that strong Republicans and conservatives were more likely to seek out information about George Bush than his opponent Al Gore (Iyengar et al. 2008).

On the other hand, recent evidence suggests that partisan selective exposure may be limited to a small, politically active subset of the population. No more than 15 percent of Americans watch cable news for more than 10 minutes per day, a number that rises only slightly during election season (Prior 2007). Whereas the relatively few highly engaged partisans may be seeking out like-minded media, "most people are news omnivores." (Sides 2013). They get their news from a variety of sources—some partisan, most not. Although heavy Fox News viewers are very loyal to their favorite network (Stroud 2011), more typical cable news viewers tune in to more than one cable outlet (Prior 2007). Even people who favor a partisan outlet as a primary source might also turn to other outlets that might offer a different perspective. According to Gentzgow and Shapiro (2011), nearly a third of people who visited Rush Limbaugh's website also visited *The New York Times* online. During the 2006 mid-term elections, a large majority of subjects in Chicago and New York showed a preference for non-partisan local news broadcasts, eschewing partisan sources altogether. Among the small minority of subjects who turned to partisan sources, only a few devoted their news exposure to one side. In short, it could be that even partisans have a "balanced news diet" (LaCour 2012).

Polarization. Another concern is that opinionated talk shows and partisan news outlets are nudging their audiences—small though they may be—toward the extremes. The logic here is that the conservative content of Fox News or Rush Limbaugh pushes its already conservative audience members further to the right; likewise for liberals watching MSNBC or reading the *Huffington Post*. If it is true that the U.S. electorate is becoming more polarized, are the new opinion-based media partly to blame? Perhaps.

Actually, there is disagreement about the extent of polarization in the general population. While there is a consensus among social scientists that Democratic and especially Republican elected officials have shifted toward the ideological extremes, ordinary citizens may have become only slightly more polarized during recent elections—if at all (Fiorina, Abrams and Pope 2006; Levendusky 2009). But remember that the audiences of opinion-based media are quite small and dominated by engaged partisans. And polarization has been evident among this subgroup of the citizenry (Abramowitz 2010).

It is easy to see how partisan media could contribute to polarization. Research on "group polarization" sheds light on how this might happen (see Stroud 2007). Under this theory, discussion or other forms of deliberative communication prompt group members to move further in the direction in which they are predisposed to lean. As a result, "groups of like-minded people, engaged in discussion with one another, end up thinking the same thing that they thought before—but in more extreme form" (Sunstein 2007: 60–61). Whereas diverse discussion networks lead to greater awareness of multiple perspectives, attitudes become polarized when people limit their deliberation to like-minded associates (Huckfeldt, Mendez, and Osborn 2004).

Polarization can occur for several reasons. For one, when a group of like-minded people discusses politics, congenial arguments will tend to outnumber counterarguments. Second, group members who are out of sync with the group will either adjust their views to more closely fit the prevailing viewpoint, or abandon the group and seek out other networks more closely aligned with their predispositions. Finally, members who are uncertain about their views on specific topics gain confidence in their predispositions after hearing or reading the opinions expressed by people like them (Sunstein 2007).

The logic of group polarization may be applied to the new media environment (Stroud 2007). Today, like-minded people can easily congregate on the air and online. Talk radio and blogs foster intra-group discussion among those who tend to agree with each other. Even with non-deliberative media such as television talk shows, group dynamics come into play because people can tune in to find out what others like them think. When the "discussion" ends, viewers are left with greater familiarity with the arguments that support their position (if not the counterarguments) and more confidence that they are right. Presumably more extreme views could follow.

Is that the case? Quite a few studies have shown that opinionated media can reinforce existing views, sometimes magnify them, and sometimes push people to the extremes. According to one set of experiments, partisan media seem to "take subjects who are already extreme and make them *even more* extreme" (Levendusky 2013: 611–612). In another, watching *Fahrenheit 9/11*, the Michael Moore documentary that mocked George W. Bush's anti-terrorism policy and therefore attracted Bush skeptics, was associated with extraordinarily unfavorable views of the President (Stroud 2007). Similarly, the anti-Clinton predispositions of Republicans in the 1990s were exacerbated among those who listened to conservative talk radio (Jones 2001). During the 1996 presidential campaign, advertising seemed more effective at reinforcing existing partisan predispositions about the candidates than changing people's minds (Kaid 1997). In Canada, a fragmented media environment seemed to magnify preexisting differences between French Quebeckers and citizens of the rest of the country (Mendelsohn and Nadeau 1996).

A polarized media environment may actually shape election results. During the early days of Fox News, towns in which a cable provider added Fox News to its channel line-up saw a small but consequential increase in Republican vote share in 1996 and 2000 (Della Vigna and Kaplan 2007). During the 2000 election, this "Fox News Effect" appeared to be concentrated among voters who were predisposed to support George W. Bush—independents and Republicans, but not Democrats (Hopkins and Ladd 2012).

Yet other studies cast serious doubt on the media's contribution to polarization. For example, innovative experiments by Arceneaux and Johnson (2013) underline the fact that cable news audiences are polarized from the start. These audiences are small, the researchers point out, and intensely partisan to begin with and therefore resistant to content that runs counter to their viewpoints. Their views do become more extreme when forced to watch programming that runs counter to their beliefs. But that rarely happens in a media environment in which people have so many options. Arceneaux and Johnson are more troubled by the ability of disengaged citizens to completely tune out the news in today's media environment than media-driven polarization.

Conservative media bubble? Even if conservative media helped George Bush in 2000, they may have hurt Mitt Romney in 2012. His defeat came as a shock to Romney and his campaign, but it should not have. Traditional news outlets reported numerous polls showing President Obama with a small but consistent lead during the final few weeks of the campaign. Why were many Republicans so surprised when the President was reelected? Partly it was the wishful thinking that accompanies any campaign. Romney campaign officials claimed that their internal polls showed a tight race in key swing states. But it also may be that by 2012, so many Republicans had abandoned traditional media outlets in favor of what GOP strategist Mike Murphy called "the conservative media bubble ... with its isolation, denial and semi-paranoia" (Burns and Martin 2012). In that bubble—which consisted of Fox News, Limbaugh, *Drudge* and other conservative outlets—audiences were told what they wanted to hear: that the polls were wrong and that Romney could still eke out a win, with some conservative commentators predicting a landslide victory for the GOP. In this partisan media cocoon, an Obama victory was difficult to imagine.

Self-destructive partisan media bubbles are not limited to conservative viewpoints. The same phenomenon could happen on the left with MSNBC and the *Huffington Post*. Democrats also seemed shocked during a key moment of the 2012 election: the first debate, when Romney came across as poised, informed and well-prepared—a sharp contrast with his Democratic opponent. This was a Romney that many of them had never seen, accustomed as they were to the negative characterizations that prevailed on both mainstream and left-leaning partisan outlets. Perhaps their own media bubble left some of them unprepared for a competent, calm Romney who suddenly seemed capable of defeating a shaky President Obama.

More Entertainment

Even with their smaller audiences, talk shows and other opinion-based outlets are popular because they entertain. Liberals enjoy watching Maddow in part because she provides an animated, sharp, sometimes funny, and certainly ideologically comfortable take on the news of the day. It is gratifying to watch a charismatic ally rip and ridicule the opposing party's positions and personalities. Limbaugh provides the same sort of satisfaction for conservatives eager to hear a well-spoken and well-informed ideological bedfellow mock President Obama and other Democrats. These outlets reassure members of their audience that their views are correct; they provide affirmation. Their hosts explain *why* their audience members' existing preferences are superior to those of the opposition. And they do so in a way that is enjoyable for people who already agree with what is being said on the air. Traditional news may be softer, punchier and perhaps more entertaining than it used to be. But it's tame stuff compared with the lively fare offered on talk radio, cable television and the blogosphere.

Late-night Comedy

Late-night comedy programs are intended to entertain, first and foremost. But in the process of amusing members of their audience, they may also inform and perhaps even shape voters' impressions of the candidates. Some of these programs are explicitly political in format and content—*The Daily Show*, for example. *Saturday Night Live* and host-centered shows such as the *Tonight Show with Jimmy Fallon* also frequently address topical issues, especially during election season.

Late-night comedy programs attract small but devoted audiences with a disproportionately large number of young people. Studies in 2000 and 2004 by the Pew Research Center for the People & the Press led some observers to fret that some young people may actually be abandoning traditional sources of election news in favor of comedy programs as *The Daily Show* and *Saturday Night Live*. Actually, what may be happening is that a small but active subset of young people is getting news from both traditional news and late-night comedy (Young and Tisinger 2006).

Comedy Central. The Daily Show, on the Comedy Central cable network, satirizes a news broadcast. It has many of the trappings of a television news program. From 1999 until 2015, it was hosted by Jon Stewart. As mock-anchor, the host orchestrates a series of brief lampooned news stories, drawing heavily on the actual news of the day. The anchor cuts away to mock-correspondents, who either pretend to report live from a news hot-spot or present a spoofed feature story during which subjects inadvertently make fools of themselves. The program not only pokes fun at the subjects of the story (usually politicians), but also journalists and the oddities of modern newsgathering (Fox News and CNN are favorite targets).

For example, on the day after the 2012 election, *The Daily Show* ridiculed Fox News for predicting that Mitt Romney would defeat Barack Obama despite polls showing the President with a solid lead. As usual, the story featured a series of clips of people saying embarrassing things—in this case, pundits like Dick Morris claiming "We're going to win by a landslide," and host Stuart Varney casting doubt on the polls by saying "You can go through all the scientific gobbly-gook you like, I don't believe 'em." Stewart then aimed his ridicule at Republican strategist and Fox News analyst Karl Rove, who is shown disputing his own network's decision to declare victory for Obama in battleground state of Ohio. When Rove explains how the state could still be won by Romney, host Megyn Kelly asks him "is this just math that you do as a Republican to make yourself feel better, or is this real?" Stewart used this as an opportunity to mock the network's "Fair and Balanced" slogan:

> By the way, "Math You Do As a Republican to Make Yourself Feel Better" is a much better slogan for Fox than the one they have now.

As this excerpt makes clear, Stewart didn't hide his left-leaning political views. And although *The Daily Show* skewers politicos of all ideological stripes, most of the ridicule is reserved for conservative politicians, activists and media.

Also on Comedy Central, *The Colbert Report*'s political bent was a bit less obvious, partly due to its format. Hosted by Stephen Colbert, the show aired from 2005 to 2014. A spoof of a talk show, it centered on Colbert's parody of a self-aggrandizing, loud-mouth conservative host. His character was loosely based on Bill O'Reilly of Fox News, whom he called "Papa Bear." Like O'Reilly, he used monologues and aggressive interviews to mock liberals and their ideas while celebrating right-leaning interests. But since Colbert was a caricature, the joke was on the causes and people he ostensibly promoted rather than the other way around.

Sometimes Colbert was surprisingly substantive. In the wake of the Supreme Court's 2010 *Citizens United* decision, Colbert used the parody to convey the effects of the ruling on campaign finance practices. In character, he did several interviews with former Federal Election Commission Chairman Trevor Potter, explaining how the ruling enabled the creation of "Super PACs"—organizations that could raise and spend unlimited money on behalf of candidates. Working with Potter, Colbert then created his own Super PAC "Americans for a Better Tomorrow, Tomorrow," which became a running gag for much of the early parts of the presidential campaign. In 2011, the Super PAC segments won a Peabody, a prestigious journalism award. According to the Peabody judges, "through inventive comedy, sight gags and mock-strident rhetoric, The Colbert Report used its 'megaphone of cash' to illuminate the far-ranging effects on our politics of the *Citizens United* decision" (Peabody Awards 2011).

Saturday Night Live. Political skits have been a mainstay of *Saturday Night Live* since the show's launch in 1975. Each 90-minute *SNL* episode features a variety of comedy sketches performed by regular cast members and special guests. The longest running recurring sketch is *Weekend Update*, a precursor to *The Daily Show* in that it lampoons television news. The format is a familiar one: a cast member (sometimes two) spoofs the role of anchor, who reads parodied news stories and interviews commentators played by cast members or special guests. The anchor role has been performed by some of the show's most famous cast members, including Tina Fey, Amy Poehler, Jimmy Fallon, and—the skit's co-creator—Chevy Chase.

Much of the show's political content centers on cast members' impersonations of politicians.

During its premiere season, a popular recurring sketch was Chase's parody of President Gerald Ford's clumsiness and propensity for verbal gaffes. In one skit, Chase spoofs a televised address by Ford from the Oval Office:

> My fellow Americans, I have called upon the networks tonight to make two pressing issues clear to the American public [sneezes and wipes nose with tie]. Number one, the possible default of New York City. And number one, my stand on the Ronald Reagan announcement.

As usual, the skit concludes with Chase falling off the set—a reference to President Ford's recent stumble and fall off the steps of Air Force One in 1975. Although Chase's running gag satirized some of Ford's foibles, he made little attempt to actually impersonate the President. He didn't modify his voice nor was his appearance altered to resemble Ford in any way. By contrast, when Dan Ackroyd played Democratic candidate Carter for a mock-debate with Chase's Ford during the 1976 election, he attempted to imitate the appearance and voice of the actual politician. Impersonation-centered political skits have since become a mainstay of political comedy on *SNL*, especially during election season. Favorites included Dana Carvey's send-up of both George H.W. Bush and independent candidate Ross Perot, and Will Ferrell's caricature of George W. Bush. But the most famous was Tina Fey's impersonation of Sarah Palin during the 2008 election.

BOX 2.1 FEY–PALIN, PALIN–FEY

Republican voters cheered when John McCain selected Sarah Palin as his running mate in August 2008. Her rousing acceptance speech at the Republican convention spurred a poll surge that virtually tied the race, at least for a few days. But by October, Palin had committed a number of gaffes and stumbled badly in televised interviews. Late-night comedians pounced.

Among them was *Saturday Night Live*'s Tina Fey, who possessed both a strong physical resemblance to Palin and a knack for mimicking her voice and mannerisms. Fey imitated Palin in six *SNL* skits during the fall campaign. In the first skit, Fey's Palin shared a podium for a joint speech with Hillary Clinton, played by fellow comedian and friend Amy Poehler. The overt message critiqued sexism in electoral politics. But the subtext was the contrast between Clinton's hard-earned political experience and Palin's shallow ignorance. The second skit was more potentially damaging to Palin. It spoofed an actual interview of Palin by Katie Couric for CBS News, during which Palin stumbled badly with uninformed and rambling answers to Couric's questions. In the skit, Fey parodied Palin's gestures and several of her odd statements. But the most biting segment was when Fey spoofed Palin's rambling, nonsensical response to Couric's question about the economic crisis and the government's $700 million bailout. In Fey's rendition, Palin responded:

> Like every American I'm speaking with, we are ill about this. We're saying, hey, why bail out Fannie and Freddie, and not me. But ultimately, what the bailout does is help those that are concerned about the health care reform that is needed to help shore up our economy. To help, um—it's gotta be all about job creation, too. Also too, shoring up our economy, and putting Fannie and Freddie back on the right track. And, so, health care reform and reducing taxes and reining in spending, 'cause, Barack Obama, you know. You know, we've got to accompany tax reduction, and tax relief for Americans. Also, having a dollar value meal at restaurants—that's gonna help. But, one in five jobs being created today, under the umbrella of job creation. That, you know, also.

A later skit parodied the debate between Palin and Joe Biden during which Fey poked fun of Palin's embrace of the label "maverick" to describe her and her running mate: "You know, John McCain and I, we're a couple of mavericks. And, gosh darnit, we're gonna take that maverick energy right to Washington and we're gonna use it to fix this financial crisis and everything else that's plaguin' this great country of ours." On the October 23rd episode, the real Palin made a guest appearance alongside Fey's mock Palin. By that time, Fey's imitation had been "so dead-on that, when the real Palin later appeared onscreen with her, it was difficult to tell who was who" (Lichter, Baumgartner and Morris 2015).

The skits coincided with Palin's decline in the polls, leading some to speculate about a negative "Fey effect" on Palin's popularity. At least one study found a connection between Fey's impersonation and younger people's impressions of Palin (Baumgartner, Morris and Walth 2012). But this was Obama's election to lose; vice presidential candidates have minimal influence on the voters' choice for president (Romero 2001). The lasting effect was that for some voters, the real Palin and Fey's Palin were indistinguishable.

Fey won an Emmy for her performance.

Late-night talk shows. The oldest form of late-night TV comedy is the talk show. Popular shows in this genre include *The Tonight Show with Jay Leno* (who replaced late-night comedy pioneer Johnny Carson), the *Late Show with David Letterman, Late Night with Jimmy Fallon,* and Conan O'Brien's *Conan.* All of these shows feature opening monologues, during which the host will tell a number of jokes drawing upon current events. During the 2012 election, for example, Jay Leno poked fun at Mitt Romney's old-fashioned sensibilities:

> During last night's debate, President Obama told Mitt Romney, "The 1980s called and they want their foreign policy back." Romney tried to deliver a comeback but then his beeper went off.

Referring to President Obama's lackluster performance in his first debate with Mitt Romney, Jimmy Fallon quipped:

> This week President Obama's Facebook page received more than a million "Likes" in a single day. All of them from Republicans who watched last week's debate.

In recent elections, late-night talk shows have provided new opportunities for candidates to reach voters. Presidential candidates are routinely invited to appear as guests, and they nearly always accept. Appearing on entertainment-oriented talk shows gives candidates a chance to showcase their sense of humor and other "human qualities" in a relatively friendly setting. The practice started during the 1992 presidential campaign, when a shades-wearing Bill Clinton played "Heartbreak Hotel" on saxophone during an appearance on the *Arsenio Hall Show.* At the time, Clinton was criticized for denigrating presidential politics with a low-brow stunt. But since then, many presidential candidates have risked potential ridicule in the hopes of reaching potential voters who might not otherwise pay much attention to other forms of campaign communication. One day after formally launching his 2016 presidential campaign, Jeb Bush starred in Fallon's recurring "slow jam the news" skit, which required that he recite talking points while the host sang lyrics that were laden with sexual innuendo. Nowadays, candidates make news when they refuse to appear on a particular show, as was the case with Mitt Romney when he repeatedly declined the invitation of David Letterman, who had been criticized by Republicans for being overly generous to Obama.

It is important to note that many viewers are not watching these shows in their entirety on television. Instead, they watch them online, often one segment or skit at a time. The programs are called "late night" because that is when they are broadcast on television. But younger people in particular watch "TV" on demand, when and where they want—on their phone, laptop or tablet; at home, in the office, or—much to their professor's dismay—during class. Some viewers might go directly to the show's website and either watch an entire episode or just pick and choose the skits that look compelling. Advertisers pay top dollar for these "views" because the consumer actively sought out the program (Weiner 2015). Many viewers will instead stumble upon a segment when a link appears on their favorite news aggregator or social media newsfeed. One indication that a political comedy skit has gone viral is if gets a headline on the front page of the *Huffington Post*. Another is if a bunch of your friends post a link to it on Facebook.

Effects of Political Comedy

In the process of amusing their audiences, late-night comedy programs may also be shaping elections and informing voters. According to a study of the 2004 election, *The Daily Show's* ridicule of George W. Bush and John Kerry was associated with less favorable audience impressions of *both* candidates—not just the Republican (Baumgartner and Morris 2006). After Bush appeared on *The Late Show with David Letterman* during the 2000 election, viewers were more likely to evaluate him based on character traits rather than his issue positions (Moy, Xenos and Hess 2005). Do *SNL's* impersonations of candidates influence voters' impressions? Tiny Fey's imitation of Sarah Palin was so pervasive in 2008 that it would not be a stretch to assume that some voters conflated the spoofed Palin with the real one. Indeed, one study found that watching Fey's impersonation was associated with declining approval of Palin and intention to vote for the GOP ticket (Baumgartner, Morris and Walth 2012).

Do viewers actually learn anything from late-night comedy? Research on daytime talk shows and other forms of "soft news" suggest that politically inattentive individuals gain enough information from programs like *The Oprah Winfrey Show* to make reasoned vote choices (Baum and Jamison 2006). These are people who do not consume much "hard news," so they stand to benefit from entertaining programming that provides at least some political content. Late-night comedy seems to attract a more politically attentive audience. Compared with viewers of similar programs, audience members of *The Daily Show* appear to be remarkably well-informed (Young and Tisinger 2006). Presumably the jokes aren't funny unless viewers already have some knowledge about the subject of the jokes. But are they better informed as a result of watching the show or because they already possessed the information? Probably the latter. Results are mixed, but on balance existing research suggests that viewers gain only a limited amount of additional knowledge from watching late-night comedy. One exception is a study showing that viewers can learn from *The Daily Show* if they are actually motivated to seek out information—gather news—rather than merely be entertained (Feldman 2013). It also may be true that late-night comedy serves as a "gateway" to traditional news sources. Even if the programs themselves do not lead to additional knowledge, they might prompt viewers to seek out more serious, information-heavy news elsewhere (Feldman and Young 2006). Presumably the results include not only more knowledge, but a better appreciation for the jokes.

Conclusion

As we have seen, the emergence of highly opinionated, entertainment-oriented media options have raised a number of concerns about where Americans get their information during elections. Academic research is helping us understand what all of this means for our electoral process. It does appear that many politically active Americans are migrating toward partisan media that reinforce rather than challenge their existing viewpoints. But partisan media do not appear to be significant contributors to political polarization.

Many citizens are getting their news from late-night comedy and other outlets that blur the line between news, opinion and entertainment. These programs can serve as a healthy informational supplement in a varied news diet. In any case, it is safe to say that talk shows, partisan news, blogs, and late-night comedy programs have invigorated elections for highly engaged citizens. And perhaps a few otherwise disengaged citizens—those who now avoid the traditional news—occasionally get sucked into the electoral process by the added entertainment value. In Chapter 5, we will turn to another relatively new type of information source: social media platforms such as Twitter and Facebook, which enable citizens to more easily share political information with each other, and thereby serve as a bridge between old and new media.

References

Abramowitz, Alan I. 2010. *The Disappearing Center: Engaged Citizens, Polarization and American Democracy*. New Haven, CT: Yale University Press.

Arceneaux, Kevin, and Martin Johnson. 2013. *Changing Minds or Changing Channels: Partisan News in an Age of Choice*. Chicago: University of Chicago Press.

Auletta, Ken 2003. "Vox Fox." *The New Yorker* (May 26): 58–73.

Baum, Matthew A., and Angela S. Jamison. 2006. "The Oprah Effect: How Soft News Helps Inattentive Citizens Vote Consistently." *Journal of Politics* 68(4): 946–959.

Baumgartner, Jody, and Jonathan Morris. 2006. "The Daily Show Effect: Candidate Evaluations, Efficacy, and American Youth." *American Politics Research* 34(3): 341–367.

Baumgartner, Jody C., Jonathan S. Morris and Natasha L. Walth. 2012. "The Fey Effect: Young Adults, Political Humor, and Perceptions of Sarah Palin in the 2008 Presidential Election Campaign." *Public Opinion Quarterly* 76(1): 95–104.

Burns, Alexander, and Jonathan Martin. 2012. "Republicans Ponder Painful Way Forward." November 8. *Politico*. http://www.politico.com/news/stories/1112/83537.html?hp=t1_3.

Coe, Kevin, David Tewksbury, Bradley J. Bond, Kristin L. Drogos, Robert W. Porter, Ashley Yahn, and Yuanyuan Zhang. 2008. "Hostile News: Partisan Use and Perceptions of Cable News Programming." *Journal of Communication* 58: 201–219.

Cunningham, Brent. 2003. "Re-Thinking Objectivity." *Columbia Journalism Review* 4 (July/August).

Della Vigna, Stefano, and Ethan Kaplan. 2007. "The Fox News Effect: Media Bias and Voting." *The Quarterly Journal of Economics* (August): 1187–1234.

Feldman, Lauren. 2013. "Learning about Politics from The Daily Show: The Role of Viewer Orientation and Processing Motivations." *Mass Communication and Society* 16(4): 586–607.

Feldman, Lauren, and Dannegal Goldthwaite Young. 2006. "Late Night Comedy as a Gateway to Traditional News: An Analysis of Trends in News Attention among Late-Night Comedy Viewers during the 2004 Presidential Primaries." *Political Communication* 25(4): 401–422.

Fiorina, Morris P., with Samuel J. Abrams and Jeremy C. Pope. 2006. *Culture War? The Myth of Polarized America.* New York: Pearson Longman.

Gentzgow, Matthew, and Jesse M. Shapiro. 2011. "Ideological Segregation Online and Offline." *Quarterly Journal of Economics* 126: 1799–1839.

Groseclose, Tim, and Jeffrey Milyo. 2005. "A Measure of Media Bias." *Quarterly Journal of Economics* 120(4): 1191–1237.

Hopkins, Daniel J., and Jonathan M. Ladd. 2012. "The Consequences of Broader Media Choice: Evidence from the Expansion of Fox News," May 29, working paper.

Huckfeldt, Robert, Paul Allen Beck, Russell J. Dalton, and Jeffrey Levine. 1995. "Political Environments, Cohesive Social Groups, and the Communication of Public Opinion." *American Journal of Political Science* 30(4): 1025–1054.

Huckfeldt, Robert, J.M. Mendez, and Tracy Osborn. 2004. "Disagreement, Ambivalence, and Engagement: the Political Consequences of Heterogeneous Networks." *Political Psychology* 25: 65–95.

Iyengar, Shanto, Kyu S. Hahn, Jon A. Krosnick, and John Walker. 2008. "Selective Exposure to Campaign Communications: The Role of Anticipated Agreement and Issue Public Membership." *Journal of Politics* 70(1): 186–200.

Iyengar, Shanto, and Kyu S. Hahn. 2009. "Red Media, Blue Media: Evidence of Ideological Selectivity in Media Use." *Journal of Communication* 59: 19–39.

Jamieson, Kathleen Hall, and Joseph N. Cappella. 2010. *Echo Chamber: Rush Limbaugh and the Conservative Media Establishment.* New York: Oxford University Press.

Jones, David A. 2001. "The Polarizing Effect of New Media Messages." *International Journal of Public Opinion Research* 14(2): 158–174.

Kaid, Lynda Lee. 1997. "Effects of Television Spots on Images of Dole and Clinton." *The American Behavioral Scientist* 40(8): 1085–1094.

LaCour, Michael J. 2012. "A Balanced News Diet, Not Selective Exposure: Evidence from a Direct Measure of Media Exposure," October 17, working paper, Department of Political Science, University of California Los Angeles.

Levendusky, Matthew. 2009. *The Partisan Sort: How Liberals Became Democrats and Conservatives became Republicans.* Chicago: University of Chicago Press.

Levendusky, Matthew W. 2013. "Why Do Partisan Media Polarize Viewers?" *American Journal of Political Science* 57(3): 611–623.

Lichter, Robert S., Jody C. Baumgartner, and Jonathan S. Morris. 2015. *Politics is a Joke: How Comedians Are Remaking Political Life.* Boulder, CO: Westview.

Mendelsohn, Matthew, and Nadeau, Richard. 1996. "The Magnification and Minimiza-tion of Social Cleavages by the Broadcast and Narrowcast News Media." *International Journal of Public Opinion Research* 8(4): 374–389.

Mitchell, Amy. 2014. "State of the News Media." Pew Research Center, March 26. http://www.journalism.org/2014/03/26/state-of-the-news-media-2014-overview/.

Mitchell, Amy, Mark Jurkowitz, and Kenneth Olmstead. 2014. "Social, Search and Direct: Pathways to Digital News." Pew Research Center, March 13: http://www.journalism.org/2014/03/13/social-search-direct/.

Moy, Patricia, Michael A. Xenos, and Verena Hess. 2005. "Priming Effects of Late-Night Comedy." *International Journal of Public Opinion Research* 18(2): 198–210.

Mutz, Diana, and Paul S. Martin. 2001. "Facilitating Communication across Lines of Political Difference: The Role of Mass Media." *American Political Science Review* 95(1): 97–114.

Peabody Awards. 2011. "The Colbert Report—Super PAC Segments (Comedy Central)," http://www.journalism.org/analysis_report/winning_media_campaign_2012.

Pew Research Center. 2012. "Winning the Media Campaign 2012," November 2, http://www.journalism.org/analysis_report/winning_media_campaign_2012.

Prior, Markus. 2007. *Post-Broadcast Democracy: How Media Choice Increases Inequality in Political Involvement and Polarizes Elections.* New York: Cambridge University Press.

Romero, David W. 2001. "Requiem for a Lightweight: Vice Presidential Candidate Evaluations and the Presidential Vote." *Presidential Studies Quarterly* 31(3): 454–463.

Schudson, Michael. 1978. *Discovering the News: A Social History of American Newspapers.* New York: Basic Books.

Sides, John. 2013. "Can Partisan Media Contribute to Healthy Politics?" *The Monkey Cage,* March 10. http://themonkeycage.org/2013/03/10/can-partisan-media-contribute-to-healthy-politics/.

Stroud, Natalie Jomini. 2007. "Media Effects, Selective Exposure, and *Fahrenheit 9/11.*" *Political Communication* 24: 415–432.

Stroud, Natalie Jomini. 2011. *Niche News: The Politics of News Choice.* New York: Oxford University Press.

Sunstein, Cass. 2007. *Republic.com 2.0.* Princeton, NJ: Princeton University Press.

Weiner, Jonah. 2015. "The Laugh Factory." *The New York Times Magazine* (June 21): 38–45, 52, 55, 57.

West, Darrell M. 2001. *The Rise and Fall of the Media Establishment.* Boston: Bedford/St. Martin's.

Young, Dannagal G., and Russell M. Tisinger. 2006. "Dispelling Late-Night Myths: News Consumption among Late-Night Comedy Viewers and the Predictors of Exposure to Various Late-Night Shows." *The Harvard International Journal of Press/Politics* 11: 113–134.

3

EARNED MEDIA

In Chapters 1 and 2, readers were given an overview of the news media and introduced to some of the alternative outlets that inform, inflame and entertain voters during election season. The next three chapters will turn to how campaigns have adapted to these massive changes with strategies that help them communicate with voters through various forms of media: earned, paid, and social. Earned media strategies are the focus of the first of these chapters.

Candidates are not helpless victims of the news media. Their campaigns have become remarkably adept at "managing the news"—or, attempting to shape news coverage to their strategic advantage. How do they do this? Several ways. They grant exclusive interviews and other forms of access to reporters and news organizations that produce stories they like, and limit access to—or simply cut off—journalists whose stories they dislike. They leak damaging information about opponents in the hopes that news organizations will air or publish the dirt. They spin poll results, debate performances and other events that are subject to interpretation and that the media are bound to analyze. They organize photo-ops in an attempt to shape the visual aspects of election news coverage. All of these efforts give campaigns a semblance of control over what is otherwise a chaotic communication process that is fraught with peril for candidates of both parties.

These techniques fall under the category of "earned media," sometimes known as media or press relations. Earned media is also called "free media" because, unlike with advertising (also known as "paid media"), campaigns don't actually buy news coverage. Paid media strategies will be analyzed in the next chapter. With their earned media strategies, campaigns attempt to garner advantageous media coverage by employing practices that account for the realities of the modern news media discussed in Chapter 1. Indeed, understanding these realities is key to a successful earned media strategy.

The term "free media" also implies that working with the news media is cost-free. That is not the case. News management requires time and effort by the candidates and their staffs. Many campaigns have at least one staff person dedicated to earned media—usually a press secretary or equivalent. Presidential and many state-wide races often have an entire department dedicated to press relations. As we have seen in Chapter 1, news coverage may also exact costs in terms of shifting issue priorities, story frames and voter attitudes. In addition, unfavorable news coverage can be psychologically costly by damaging the morale of the candidate, the staff and volunteers. That is partly because efforts to shape news coverage often fall short. Indeed, earned media strategies may be more sophisticated than ever, but they don't always work. They make up just one of many factors that shape election news coverage. Ultimately, it is journalists, editors and producers who make editorial decisions, often leaving the campaigns disappointed—and sometimes infuriated—by the stories the media produce.

Earned Media Tools

Campaigns employ a variety of standard tools as part of their earned media efforts. Under the leadership of a press secretary or equivalent, they write press releases; host photo ops, press conferences and other media events; and grant interviews to individual reporters. Before analyzing broader earned media strategies, it is useful to review these tools.

Press secretaries interact with the media on behalf of the campaign. Their job is to handle inquiries from reporters, explain the candidate's schedule, and strategically feed information to news outlets (Semiatin 2004). They oversee the production of press releases and other materials supplied to the media. Sometimes they will grant reporters' requests for "face time" with the candidate; more often than not, however, they will handle the questions themselves, speaking on behalf of the candidate. They guide the candidate through press conferences and other media events. When a scandal erupts or gaffe is uttered, it is the press secretary who cleans up the media side of the mess. According to political scientist Richard Semiatin (2004), their styles range from conciliatory to combative. Conciliatory press secretaries maintain a positive, sometimes friendly relationship with reporters, whereas their combative counterparts see reporters as adversaries and act accordingly.

Not all campaigns can afford a press secretary; campaigns for down-ballot races might rely on the campaign manager or other senior staffer to liaise with the press. By contrast, presidential campaigns have the resources to divide these responsibilities among more than one staffer, including a traveling press secretary who handles day-to-day interactions with the media.

Press releases are campaign-prepared documents that mimic news stories. Like newspaper articles, they usually contain a headline and an introductory "lede" that introduces the key aspects of the story. They are written in the same "inverted pyramid" style that journalists employ, with the most important information emphasized at the beginning followed by additional material in order of diminishing importance. Press releases also might contain direct quotes from the candidate and other sources within the campaign. They are often accompanied by a photo or video link.

Campaigns use press releases to:

- Announce and provide details about upcoming campaign events.
- Respond to attacks by opposing candidates or groups.
- Provide the media with the candidate's position on an issue or event that is making news.
- Help do "damage control" when a controversy erupts

The simulated-journalism format reflects the (usually fruitless) hope that news organizations will simply run the press release as is. But the truth is, many press releases end up in the recycling bin; ditto for electronic versions sent by email. Even so, some resource-strapped media outlets rely heavily on press releases for both text and visuals. A reporter who is pressed for time or access can use the direct quotes or factual information provided in the release. Even journalists who roll their eyes at press releases might read them anyway to get a sense of what campaigns are prioritizing and how they are responding to changing events. Then they may use the contact information provided at the top of the release to do their own reporting.

Interviews are essential to election reporting. Reporters use these question-and-answer sessions to gain background knowledge, collect factual information and gather direct quotes for their stories. Sometimes the candidate is the subject of the interview; more often the subject is the press secretary or other member of the campaign staff. Most interviews are conducted informally over the phone or by email. But occasionally a campaign will allow a reporter to conduct a face-to-face interview with the candidate. When granted to a television news outlet, an interview may be taped and included as part of a news story or shown on its own.

Candidates are coached to answer reporters' questions carefully. Reporters will use interviews to ask probing questions about subjects that matter to them: controversies, the horse race, areas of conflict, past mistakes. A candidate might prefer to field questions about tax reform; the reporter is probably more interested in discussing a gaffe the candidate made last week or why the candidate is 10 points behind in the polls. Press secretaries prepare their candidates to answer questions about all three subjects, and coach them on how to turn the conversation toward favorable policy-related topics.

In 2008, Republican vice presidential nominee Sarah Palin was famously unprepared for a series of interviews with CBS News anchor Katie Couric. Palin had stumbled a few weeks earlier in an interview with ABC News' Charles Gibson, highlighted by the claim that her home state of Alaska's proximity to Russia strengthened her foreign policy credentials. This mild blunder became a famous gaffe when *Saturday Night Live* comedian Tina Fey, imitating Palin, spoofed the claim with the line, "I can see Russia from my house!" (see Box 2.1). But the interviews with Couric were a complete disaster. When Couric asked Palin to provide examples of her running mate John McCain's efforts to boost oversight of Wall Street, she replied "I'll try to find some and bring them to you." When questioned about the relevance of Russia's proximity to Alaska, she replied, "As Putin rears his head and comes into the airspace of the United States of America, where do they go? It's Alaska." (Heilemann and Halperin 2010: 399). Palin was unable to name newspapers she read or Supreme Court cases that she disagreed with besides *Roe v. Wade*. The interview provides a cautionary case study of what happens when a candidate fails to prepare for interactions with the news media.

It is up to the campaigns to establish the ground rules on sourcing and attribution before the interview begins. Reporters prefer that interviews be "on the record," which means that all that is said can be quoted directly in the story and attributed to the source. But for strategic purposes, a source might prefer to speak "off the record," which means no direct quotes and no source attribution. Variations of the latter include "not for attribution," which allows the reporter to use a direct quote as long as the source is described in generic terms ("a campaign spokes-person," for example); "on background," which disallows both specific sourcing and direct quotes; and "deep background," which limits use of the information to enhancing the reporter's understanding of the subject.

Candidates and staffers sometimes learn the hard way that unless they are explicit about sourcing, reporters will assume they are speaking on the record. Mary Matalin, Deputy Campaign Manager for President George H.W. Bush's 1992 reelection campaign, was not explicit in a conversation with veteran reporter Jules Witcover about what she perceived as a moderating of the rhetoric about the abortion issue. To embellish her point, she said "You don't see 'fetuses,' you don't see 'hangers' dominating the debate." Unfortunately for Matalin, Witcover printed the comment verbatim, and it became the "Quote of the Day" in *Hotline*, a daily newsletter widely circulated among political junkies. When Matalin called Witcover to complain, he replied: "You know the rules. You should have said 'I'm on background'" (Matalin and Carville 1995: 177).

Press conferences provide a means of consolidating interviews. Instead of meeting face-to-face with one reporter, press conferences allow the candidate to answer questions from a larger group of reporters simultaneously. A typical press con-ference begins with a prepared statement from the candidate, who then opens the floor to questions from the reporters. The candidate calls on reporters individually—by name, if they are prepared—which means the candidate determines which news outlets get their questions asked. As with interviews, candidates are coached to answer a wide array of questions—some friendly, most not. But since the questions are coming from so many different reporters, it is even more difficult to anticipate the nature of the questions. Even reporters who are perceived as friendly to the campaign may surprise the candidate with a tough "gotcha" or "zinger" question. Press conferences may be an efficient means of reaching a wide array of media outlets, but they can be very unpredictable. As a result, many campaigns avoid them.

Photo-ops and other media events give campaigns more control in part because reporters play a relatively passive role. Short for "photo opportunity," these events are staged by the campaign to give news organizations the visuals they need without sacrificing the campaign's desire for control. Photos and video are the focus; rarely are reporters allowed to ask more than a few questions, if any at all. Campaigns use photo-ops to reinforce their strategic aims. Sometimes they underline the campaign's "message of the day"; other times they highlight an issue priority. For example, a campaign seeking to shore up support among pro-gun voters might invite news outlets to join the candidate for target practice at a local shooting range. The campaign's objective is that subsequent news coverage be accompanied by a photo or video clip of the candidate taking a shot while spectators cheer her on. Reporters may chafe at the perceived manipulation, but the photo runs anyway because the visuals are dramatic.

Some photo-ops are more successful than others. In 1992, Democratic running mates Bill Clinton and Al Gore spent much of July and August on bus tours of key battleground states. Along the way, they stopped at factories, meet-and-greets, potluck dinners, and even a miniature golf course—all with reporters and cameras in tow. Initially positive, the national media got bored with the story once the novelty wore off. But for local news outlets, it was big news when the bus came to town, sometimes resulting in hours of live coverage and front-page stories in the local paper. A *New York Times* reporter called it a "free commercial on wheels" because of the fawning local media coverage (Berke 1992).

A less successful photo-op was staged by Al Gore's presidential campaign seven years later. As intended, a casually dressed Gore was depicted paddling a canoe down the Connecticut River. But Gore appeared stiff to some reporters, and the visuals were overshadowed when a controversy erupted over the local utility's decision to pour millions of gallons of water in the drought-depleted river to save Gore from the embarrassment of running aground (Henneberger 1999). Needless to say, the headline "Gore's canoe was kept afloat by water from dam"[1] did not reinforce Gore campaign's message of the day. An event that was supposed to loosen Gore's image and underline his environmental record instead underscored the perception that the campaign was struggling.

Other photo-ops are simply part of the campaign's "retail" effort. Retail campaigning involves face-to-face interaction between the candidate and voters— "shaking hands and kissing babies," "pressing the flesh," and "going door to door." Retail may be old-fashioned and time-consuming but it is the single most effective way for a candidate to secure individual votes (Burton and Shea 2010). When the media cover a candidate interacting with voters, retail merges with "wholesale" (campaigning that reaches large numbers of voters at the same time).

Campaign rallies are designed to fire up supporters, but they also attract news coverage by local media. The retail effort also includes the candidate's participation in public events such as holiday parades, barbecues, harvest festivals and church picnics. By encouraging reporters, photographers and camera crews to follow the candidate around, a campaign can extend the candidate's reach beyond the voters who attend the event.

The campaign's "advance team" is crucial to the success of campaign events. Its job is to arrive early, scout the location, and choreograph the visual aspects of the event so that the candidate's image is maximized on television and in photos. Every detail is important: the demographic characteristics of the attendees; the position of the sun; the size of the room. A successful advance effort results in a mix of races and ages in the audience; candidates who aren't forced to squint because the sun is in their eyes; a packed room full of cheering supporters. When Mitt Romney ran for president in 2012, his advance team was considered a well-oiled machine (Parker 2012). But during the Republican primaries, Romney was stuck addressing the 1,200-member Detroit Economic Club in a 65,000-seat football stadium. The club took responsibility for the scheduling snafu, and the Romney campaign nearly salvaged the event by situating camera crews behind the candidate so that the backdrop would be filled with members of the audience. That worked fine until reporters Tweeted photos taken from an angle showing Romney speaking to a nearly empty stadium. The day got worse when Romney, departing from script, mentioned that his wife "drives a couple of Cadillacs," reinforcing his image as a tone-deaf wealthy plutocrat.

BOX 3.1 DAMAGE CONTROL

When a candidate makes a gaffe or scandal breaks, what follows is what political scientist Larry Sabato calls a media "feeding frenzy"—that is, "press coverage attending any political event or circumstance where a critical mass of journalists leap to cover the same embarrassing or scandalous subject and pursue it intensely, often excessively, and sometimes uncontrollably" (Sabato 1993: 6). What might campaigns do to limit the damage? Campaign professionals offer a number of recommendations:

- *Do counter-opposition research.* Whereas opposition research digs up dirt on opponents, counter-"oppo" helps campaigns anticipate their own candidate's vulnerabilities before they make news. Counter-opposition research should offer frank assessments of the candidate's problematic voting records, newsworthy marital problems or other family difficulties, and sticky financial decisions—any potential weakness that might make news (or appear on an opponent's attack ad). This information enables campaigns to prepare responses to media inquiries in advance, and react quickly if and when news breaks.

- *Get out front.* If possible, candidates should respond to the crisis on the same day as the original report. Usually reporters will seek the campaign's response before the news outlet runs the story. Take advantage of this opportunity to compress the breaking news and the campaign's response into one news cycle. Delayed, tentative reactions magnify the tendency for feeding frenzies to last for days if not weeks.
- *Be consistent.* Campaigns should make sure that initial response is a good one because changing messages signals desperation and uncertainty. When campaigns shift gears without explanation, their strategic failure can become its own damaging story.
- *Don't lie or cover up.* It is nearly impossible to get away with a falsehood in today's media environment. Although traditional reporting resources have been depleted, bloggers and advocacy groups compensate with their own investigations. In the media's eyes, getting caught lying about a controversy is sometimes worse than the original misdeed.
- *Apologize if warranted.* Sometimes it makes sense for the candidate to fess up and apologize. Candidates are reluctant to do this because it signals weakness. But if the charges are correct and the feeding frenzy won't fade otherwise, candidates might be better off apologizing to affected parties: voters, supporters, staffers, family members, etc. An apology may not end the story, but it can reveal human qualities that may limit the damage.

Sources: Sabato (1993); Matalin and Carville (1995); Powell and Cowart (2003)

Earned Media Strategies

Journalists resent photo ops. They see them as contrived, manipulative and sometimes downright silly. Although rallies and other events provide sought-after visuals, they lack the conflict and drama that make an ideal story. "If everyone is cheering for the candidate, nobody is arguing" (Sides et al. 2014: 204). Ditto for press releases, which reporters pretend to ignore (but sometimes use to save time or compensate for the dearth of information from the campaign). Interviews and press conferences are preferable because reporters lead the questioning, and candidates are more likely to make news with their answers (especially if they make a gaffe). But many candidates avoid them.

Even so, these earned media devices persist because they serve the needs of both campaigns and news outlets. A media event may lack new information, but it "is concrete and discrete; ordinarily it can be explained clearly in a limited time and space" (Jamieson and Campbell 1997: 46). Campaigns may resent the news media, but they remain key sources of election information for voters. It is thus in the interest of campaigns to maintain a cooperative, working relationship with the news media. Journalists may resent the self-serving nature of campaigns' earned media efforts, but they depend on them to get the information, quotes, and visuals they need in a timely manner. The next section turns to the broader strategies campaigns employ to foster a working relationship that results in less negative news coverage than would otherwise be the case. Some entail cooperation between the campaign and reporters; others reflect the tension that so often underlies this relationship.

"Going Local" and Other Media Avoidance Strategies

Some campaigns reject the above premise and opt to avoid traditional news media as much as possible. This approach is becoming increasingly common for Republicans fed up with the so-called "liberal media." To many Republicans, the "Washington media" are not worth the bother; they assume the Democratic candidate will get far more favorable treatment regardless of what they do. Instead they focus their media outreach efforts on ideologically friendly talk radio programs and other conservative media outlets such as Fox News and its roster of right-leaning talk show hosts. In 2012, the Romney campaign eschewed press conferences in favor of one-on-one interviews on Fox News. Romney adviser Eric Fehrnstrom explained:

> We'd much rather go on a Fox program where we know the question is going to come up and Mitt can give his answer and it's not going to a frenzy of questioning … He will be able to give his response. There may be a follow up or two, and then that's it. The frenzy is not something that you would willingly do if you had other options. It's like here you can either do this frenzied news conference, or we can do a more sedate studio appearance with Sean Hannity. I'd take the sedate over the frenzy any day.
>
> *(Hamby 2013: 50)*

His running mate, Paul Ryan, did not host a single press conference with national media during the entire campaign (Hamby 2013).

In 2014, when economics professor David Brat challenged House Majority Leader Eric Cantor for the Republican nomination in Virginia's 7th Congressional district, Brat secured endorsements from talk radio hosts Laura Ingraham, Mark Levin and Glenn Beck, and appeared on all three of their programs. Analysts credited these talk show hosts for propelling Brat to his shocking victory over the Majority Leader (Peters 2014).

Republicans are not the only candidates who avoid national reporters. It was Democrat Bill Clinton who pioneered daytime talk show appearances as a means of reaching new voters and bypassing the Washington media (see Chapter 2). Frustrated with the negativity of national news, the Clinton–Gore campaign reached out to local news outlets, granting exclusive interviews to them while spurning national media. Hillary Clinton employed a "going local" strategy when she launched her 2016 campaign for the Presidency, focusing her media outreach on local news outlets in early primary states.

Why do candidates go local? Local news coverage is seen as relatively positive and deferential to the candidates. Interview questions from local reporters tend to be softer and cover familiar topics. Whereas the national reporters have heard the candidate's stump speech dozens of times and no longer consider it news, the speech and all its trappings are deemed newsworthy by local news outlets. After all, it is big news when a presidential candidate comes to town.

At least one national news outlet—the Associated Press (AP)—reaches both local and national audiences. The AP supplies news content to 1,400 local newspapers and thousands of television and radio broadcasters. Its stories appear on the front pages of newspapers across the country, especially now that newsrooms lack the staff to supply the content on their own. By focusing their national media outreach on the AP, campaigns reach local audiences as well. According to one strategist for the 2012 Obama campaign, "We always took the AP more seriously ... As newspapers, especially regional papers, cut down on staff, you'd be amazed if you looked at it. Everyone's got the AP wire on their front page" (Hamby 2013: 70–71).

Going local makes sense for presidential candidates and even candidates in competitive state-wide races. The problem for non-presidential campaigns is that although local newspaper coverage remains a vital—yet shrinking—medium for reaching voters, local television no longer covers elections in a meaningful way. For candidates running for an office other than governor or president, the only sure guaranteed way to reach television viewers is through paid advertising (Chapter 4). Local news outlets tend to offer very little election news—unless a presidential candidate comes to town.

Controlling Access

The strategy of granting exclusive interviews to certain reporters and isolating others reflects the importance of reporters' *access* to the candidate. This is one area where campaigns have almost complete control. For example, New Jersey Governor Chris Christie has what he calls a "penalty box." It describes when reporters who cover him are "briefly shut out from the inner circle for writing something Team Christie hates" (Katz 2013). It is a weapon for campaigns, and its power resides in the need for reporters to have access to the candidate for interviews. When reporters lose access, they are less capable of doing their jobs. This hurts both the reporters and the news organizations they serve.

This happened to NBC News' Alexandra Pelosi (daughter of former House Speaker Nancy Pelosi) when she covered George W. Bush's campaign in 2000. Her friendly, jokey relationship with Bush is portrayed in *Journeys with George*, a documentary she filmed with a camcorder as she and other members of the traveling press corps followed the candidate from state to state. The chumminess broke down when Pelosi asked Bush, then governor of Texas, a tough question about the number of executions in his state. The Bush campaign responded by temporarily cutting off Pelosi's access to the candidate; Bush chided her for posing a "below the belt" question. Until access was restored, Pelosi was unable to fully do her job. This put NBC News at a competitive disadvantage compared with other news outlets covering the campaign.

Bush's opponent for the Republican nomination was Senator John McCain—the "media darling," according to the Bush campaign. This was no myth: McCain did enjoy more positive media coverage than Bush during the 2000 Republican primaries (Farnsworth and Lichter 2011), perhaps in part because he made himself so accessible to reporters. McCain's willingness to bluntly answer questions from reporters and voters was epitomized by the name of his campaign bus: the Straight Talk Express. But when McCain successfully secured the Republican nomination eight years later, his relationship with the media had soured. Like many GOP candidates, he gravitated toward limited access, shutting out media outlets perceived as being unfriendly (including *The Daily Show*, where McCain had once been a regular guest).

In 2012, neither Barack Obama nor Mitt Romney gave much access to reporters. Obama got plenty of media coverage in his capacity as President, so granting a press "avail" (short for availability) to reporters covering the campaign was more trouble than it was worth. The Romney campaign distrusted the media from Day One, and the Obama campaign's little-to-no-access strategy gave the Romney people an excuse to cut off the media as well (Hamby 2013).

Spinning the News

Chapter 1 described the long-standing trend toward analysis and interpretation in the news. Campaign professionals are well aware of the tendency, and have adapted by fine-tuning the practice of *spin*. The word "spin" has become a cliché as its popular meaning includes any form of manipulative communication. But spin can be a useful concept in political communication when the definition is narrowed to describe *strategic attempts to influence the journalistic analysis of political events*. Campaigns practice spin because if they don't, someone else—a journalist, an opponent—will determine how events are interpreted. A story reporting the latest poll results won't be limited to the raw numbers; it will also analyze why Candidate A is ahead and what Candidate B is doing to catch up. Knowing that the reporter writing the story will seek reactions, representatives from both campaigns will make themselves available as sources, prepared to spin the story's interpretation of the poll results. Candidate B's spin might critique the methodology of the poll, or point to evidence that its standing has improved. Candidate A's spin could use the opportunity to elaborate on its strategic advantages. The bottom line: the reporter needs reactions in the form of direct quotes, and the campaigns take advantage of this need to shape the story's analysis.

Debate coverage is ripe for spin. Naturally, news stories about debates cover not only what the candidates said, but also analyze how well the candidates performed and the implications of each candidate's performance for the state of the horse race. Knowing this, the candidates, press secretaries and other campaign representatives make themselves available for interviews both before and after the event. The practice has become so common that debate organizers routinely set up a "spin room," an area where campaign surrogates and reporters gather for quick interviews. This enables reporters to conduct dozens of interviews in a short amount of time; TV correspondents can easily report live reactions from the site of the debate. Campaigns like spin rooms because they can reach as many news outlets as possible. The spin room is the location of many post-debate reports on television.

A key element of spin is *managing expectations*. That usually means keeping expectations low so that they are easier to exceed. Campaigns for candidates who are weak debate performers attempt to set low expectations about how well their candidate will perform. That way if the candidate merely beats those low expectations, they can declare victory in their post-debate spin. Surrogates to a candidate who has performed well in past debates also might set low expectations in case their candidate underperforms. During the 2004 presidential election, Democrat John Kerry was seen as the stronger debater. A *Daily Show* episode parodied two reporters falling for the expectations-related spin of the campaigns they are covering:

HOST JON STEWART: How are people in the Kerry camp feeling tonight?

KERRY CAMPAIGN CORRESPONDENT ED HELMS: Ecstatic, John, Kerry's people couldn't be happier. Their candidate went up against a sitting war president who has never lost a debate, and held his own.

STEWART: Rob, what's the mood over there in the Bush camp?

BUSH CAMPAIGN CORRESPONDENT ROB CORDDRY: Triumph, John, orgasmic triumph. Their man faced off against John Kerry, a golden-tongued virtuoso of words. Captain of the Yale debate team, he's been honing his oratorical skills since the age of three. The way they see it, by not allowing himself to be reduced to tears, the President was a big winner tonight.

HELMS: If I could just interject here…

STEWART: Yes, Ed Helms…

HELMS: The Kerry campaign would like to remind America the Senator was raised in France by a pack of homosexual billionaires, and going into this had little chance against a plain-speaking hard-working man of the people like George Bush. So for Kerry to be even close in this debate they say is a huge victory.

CORDDRY: If I may, John, that's a bit of a stretch. The Bush people would like to remind everyone their man held his own against what they call the smartest man in the history of the world…

In other words, both candidates declared victory by beating expectations that had been strategically lowered by their own campaigns.

Leaking Information

Reporters depend on *news leaks* and campaigns are eager to oblige. A news leak is a behind-the-scenes, off-the-record disclosure of information to media outlets. Campaigns leak information to the media for a variety of strategic purposes. But these internally sanctioned strategic leaks should not be confused with unauthorized news leaks by a "whistleblower" aiming to expose wrongdoing from within a campaign, government agency or company. Perhaps the most famous example of an unauthorized leak was military analyst Daniel Ellsburg's secret release to *The New York Times* of the "Pentagon Papers," a classified government report on government decision-making about the Vietnam War. Similarly, the organization WikiLeaks collects top-secret government documents, classified information and other leaks from anonymous sources and posts them online for public and media consumption. Like the government, campaigns also get hit by unauthorized leaks, such as when disgruntled former staffers of Hillary Clinton's 2008 presidential campaign shared internal emails and memos to a reporter from *The Atlantic* who was writing a post-mortem on the failed campaign (Green 2008). More recently, the campaign for Democratic Senate candidate Michelle Nunn stumbled when a staffer accidently leaked internal strategy memos outlining the candidate's perceived weaknesses (Altman 2014).

Strategic leaks are also secretive, but they are authorized by the campaign. One strategy is to use leaks to launch "trail balloons" in order to gauge how voters might react to specific actions. If, for example, a candidate is mulling over whether to take a potentially controversial policy position, the campaign might take a tentative first step by leaking the possible decision to a single news outlet. A subsequent news story might read something like, "According to a campaign source, Candidate A is embracing a hard-line approach on gun control ..." If the leaked policy position is well-received by voters, then the campaign may decide it is safe to make the information official. But if controversy erupts, the campaign is in a position to distance itself from the leaked information since it was never officially announced.

Campaigns also use leaks to circulate damaging information about their opponent. Campaigns routinely conduct what is called *opposition research*—the collection and analysis of useful information about an opponent's public and sometimes private record. "Oppo" provides fodder for attack ads, direct mail, and other campaign materials. But it also dovetails with news media's preference for stories that entail controversy and scandal. And because reporting resources are stretched so thin, journalists depend on leaked opposition research for story ideas, background information, and sometimes original sources. Traditionally, when a campaign leaks oppo to a reporter, the news outlet scrutinizes the information by cross-checking with other sources and applying other fundamental reporting and fact-checking practices. Today, however, these standards are often compromised by the "need for speed" and hyper-competition between media outlets. Oppo frequently makes news before it is thoroughly checked out. And because the information was anonymously leaked rather than officially released, the source of link—the campaign itself—need not claim responsibility.

Sometimes oppo leaks backfire. The 1992 Clinton campaign thought it had struck media gold when it stumbled upon a videotaped news story reporting that Bush campaign signs were being manufactured in Brazil. Campaign manager James Carville "leaked it like a sieve" to Susan Zirinsky of CBS News (Matalin and Carville 1995: 430). This sounded like a perfect story to Carville: "Think of it: With millions of Americans out of work the President of the United States was taking his business to South America, undercutting American jobs. Is this the man you want in charge of your economy?" (Matalin and Carville 1995: 430). But the story died when the Bush campaign claimed that an independent operative paid for the materials himself without its knowledge. The Clinton campaign's credibility took a hit, as did the personnel hours spent investigating and brainstorming on a controversy that barely caused a ripple.

Choosing Topics

As we saw in Chapter 1, news outlets are more likely to cover the horse race aspects of campaigns than the candidate's policies and platforms. Although candidates would prefer to turn the focus onto their plans for government, smart campaigns adapt to the media's obsession with who is up, who is down and what both sides are doing to win. According to Democratic media consultant John Rowley:

> Candidates, as a result, are supplying more press releases about polls and fewer positive policy proposals. Candidates who offer new ideas are continually punished with scant coverage of their proposals or by being patently ignored. If candidates are rewarded by talking strategy and attacking the opposition, this is what more candidates will do.
>
> (Powell and Cowart 2003: 207)

Similarly, contrast is more compelling to the media than areas of agreement. Conflict between two or more sides is a good story by journalistic standards. According to Democratic communications strategist Anita Dunn, "A policy speech is unlikely to receive much coverage unless it contains an attack on the opponent, and the more strident or negative the attack, the more likely it is to be covered" (Dunn 1994: 120). Thus, part of an earned media strategy is writing speeches and making remarks that magnify—rather than minimize—contrasts with opponents.

It is also important to save big stories for optimal times. Politician and campaign expert Catherine Shaw tells a story about a state legislator who was being interviewed about the retirement of a veteran politician who had served in the state senate for 30 years. During the interview, the legislator announced his plans to run for his colleague's seat in the upper chamber. This candidacy launch should have been big news, but instead it was buried in a story about his senior colleague's retirement. "If the candidate had waited even one day, his announcement would have received front-page coverage" (Shaw 2014: 207).

Demonstrating Viability

Except for presidential elections, non-competitive races get very little news coverage. Incumbent candidates usually benefit because they can make news simply doing their jobs as elected officials. This is a tough situation for challengers who are perceived as hopeless. According to communications expert Anita Dunn, "[t]he decision is made (based on prior election results, money in bank, general perception), that there is no story, therefore there is no coverage, and the initial decision becomes a self-fulfilling prophecy" (Dunn 1994: 116). She tells challengers that they can count on only four stories in the local media: "their announcement, their primary victory, a general profile at some point during the campaign, and their loss" (Dunn 1994: 115–116).

Challengers in this situation must convince reporters they can pull off an upset win. Whereas a hopeless candidate is a non-story, few reporters can resist an underdog who is surging in polls against an establishment candidate. Strategists thus advise challengers to help journalists with their horse race reporting by supplying them with favorable internal polling data and impressive fundraising figures. Recognizing that news outlets like stories about campaign strategy, they can fill reporters in on *how* they plan to come from behind through their innovative ground game, microtargeted advertising, or high-profile endorsements. News outlets will cover longshot candidates as long as they have a good story to tell and a viable plan for winning.

Care and Feeding

One of the press secretary's responsibilities is to help reporters get the information they need in a timely manner. Press conferences, photo-ops and media events should be scheduled early enough to accommodate print deadlines and evening news broadcast schedules. Even though press releases almost never run as is, it is important to circulate them early enough for news outlets to use the information being provided.

On the campaign trail, media operations for presidential campaigns literally "care and feed" the reporters and camera crews assigned to cover them. As a pack, the journalists travel together on a bus and plane, sharing meals and sometimes accommodations as they follow the candidate from event to event. Rather than have journalists make their own travel arrangements, the campaigns hire the buses and planes and arrange for many of the meals, then seek reimbursement from the news outlets. That way the media are present to cover every speech, photo-op and media event. Press secretaries serve on the front lines of this "care and feeding" effort. It is their job to deal with reporters' complaints about the lack of access to the candidate, the superficial nature of the events they are expected to cover, and the bland food served on the press bus.

Some campaigns are better at the care and feeding than others. The relationship between reporters and the Romney campaign was notoriously acrimonious, largely because the campaign allowed so little direct access to the candidate. Logistics also were a problem, especially compared with the completion. After a reporter assigned to the Romney campaign peeled off to cover the President for a few days, he observed this about the Obama reelection campaign:

> I got a schedule that was like, "Here is where we are going to be between 6 and 8, and here's where you can file for your morning shows, and then we are going to be in the air for these hours and then we are going to be wheels down by 4:00, so you can track, and here's what your stand up location will look like at 6:30, here's how big the crowd is going to be, the president is going to finish either before you go on the air or start after …" And it's all laid out every morning. The Romney campaign could have cared less about that shit.
>
> *(Hamby 2013: 71)*

Clearly the Romney campaign had written off many members of press. The Obama team didn't like reporters much either, nor did they grant much access to the President. But at least in terms of logistics, its press operation ran more smoothly.

Conclusion

Reporters do not like being handled. Blatant efforts by campaigns to "manage the news" trigger resentment, animosity and eye-rolling. Yet reporters depend on campaigns for the information and access they need to produce news stories on the election.

Campaigns have learned to take advantage of this need. Some news outlets are friendlier than others, so campaigns grant more access to reporters who are less likely to produce hard-hitting coverage (local journalists, for example). Election news stories are more analytical than they used to be, so campaigns have learned to shape that analysis through spin. Stories about the horse race are more appealing than policy-based coverage, so campaigns supply and manipulate information about polls, fundraising, and strategy. News operations are increasingly under-resourced, so campaigns help time-strapped reporters do their jobs through "care and feeding" strategies. Negative campaign news prevails, especially if a scandal is involved, so campaigns do their part by leaking opposition research and other damaging information about their opponents. Such blatant efforts to manipulate coverage may irritate and annoy reporters, but reporters need the campaigns as much as the campaigns need the press. That is especially true now that news operations are cutting staff while competing with alternative media outlets for the eyes and ears of audiences—and the attention of the campaigns themselves.

But as we have seen in this chapter, earned media strategies often fall short. Candidates get hammered in the news despite the campaign's efforts to foster positive press. Local reporters sometimes write a hard-hitting piece on a Presidential candidate. Fox News sometimes surprises Republican contenders with tough "gotcha" questions during live interviews. Photo ops backfire, interviews spiral out of control, and reporters grumble—and sometimes Tweet—about the lousy food served on the press bus. Republican candidates may complain loudest about media biases, but Democratic campaigns also resent the news media for being so negative, intrusive, and focused on trivial mistakes. In the "War Room," a documentary about the 1992 Presidential campaign, Clinton campaign manager James Carville goes on an expletive-filled rant about the media's "double standard" treatment of his candidate compared with President Bush. As part of the rant, he half-jokingly implies that reporters were gun-shy with Bush because his campaign manager gets them tickets to the opera. Care and feeding indeed.

The truth is, earned media is fraught with uncertainty. Campaigns are rarely happy with the news coverage they earn. The next chapter turns to paid media strategies—advertising—which affords nearly complete control over the content and presentation of information and imagery. But as we will see, that level of control consumes a huge percentage of a campaign's budget. Social media, the subject of Chapter 5, boast qualities of paid and earned media, and may partly compensate for the shortcomings of both.

Note

1   "Gore's canoe kept afloat by water from dam." *Lubbock Avalanche-Journal*, July 24, 1999. http://lubbockonline.com/stories/072499/nat_0724990090.shtml

References

Altman, Alex. 2014. "Michelle Nunn's Leaked Memos Offer Rare Glimpse of Campaign Calculation." *Time*, July 28. http://time.com/3047559/michelle-nunn-leaked-campaign-memo-georgia/.

Berke, Richard L. 1992. "THE 1992 CAMPAIGN: The Media; Clinton Bus Tour Woos and Wows Local Press." *The New York Times*, August 9. http://www.nytimes.com/1992/08/09/us/the-1992-campaign-the-media-clinton-bus-tour-woos-and-wows-local-press.html.

Burton, Michael John, and Daniel M. Shea. 2010. *Campaign Craft: The Strategies, Tactics, and Art of Political Campaign Management*. New York: Praeger.

Dunn, Anita. 1994. "The Best Campaign Wins: Local Press Coverage of Nonpresidential Races." *Campaigns and Elections American Style*, ed. James A. Thurber and Candice J. Nelson. Boulder, CO: Westview.

Farnsworth, Stephen J., and S. Robert Lichter. 2011. *The Nightly News Nightmare: Media Coverage of U.S. Presidential Elections, 1988–2008*, 3rd edition. Lanham, MD: Rowman & Littlefield.

Green, Joshua. 2008. "The Front-Runner's Fall." *The Atlantic*, Sept. 1. http://www.theatlantic.com/magazine/archive/2008/09/the-front-runner-s-fall/306944/.

Hamby, Peter. 2013. "Did Twitter Kill the Boys on the Bus? Searching for a Better Way to Cover a Campaign." Discussion Paper Series #D-80, Joan Shorenstein Center on the Press, Politics and Public Policy, Boston, MA. http://shorensteincenter.org/wp-content/uploads/2013/08/d80_hamby.pdf.

Heilemann, John, and Mark Halperin. 2010. *Game Change: Obama and the Clintons, McCain and Palin, and the Race of a Lifetime*. New York: Harper.

Henneberger, Melinda. 1999. "Gore Takes Aw-Shucks Tour (and Hits a Bump)." *The New York Times*, July 24. http://www.nytimes.com/1999/07/24/us/gore-takes-aw-shucks-tour-and-hits-a-bump.html.

Jamieson, Kathleen Hall, and K.K. Campbell. 1997. *The Interplay of Influence: News, Advertising, Politics and the Mass Media*, 4th edition. Belmont, CA: Wadsworth.

Katz, Matt. 2013. "Extremely Loud and Incredibly Close: The Strange Thrill of Covering Chris Christie." *PoliticoMagazine*, November 25. http://www.politico.com/magazine/story/2013/11/extremely-loud-and-incredibly-close-chris-christie-campaign-diary-99664.html#.VYmi9mONeoo.

Matalin, Mary, and James Carville. 1995. *All's Fair: Love, War and Running for President*. New York: Simon & Schuster.

Parker, Ashley. 2012. "Romney Advance Team Works Every Angle in Pursuit of Visual Perfection." *The New York Times*, November 1. http://www.nytimes.com/2012/11/02/us/politics/romneys-advance-team-tirelessly-pursues-perfection.html?pagewanted=all.

Peters, Jeremy W. 2014. "Potent Voices of Conservative Media Propelled Cantor Opponent." *The New York Times*, June 11. http://www.nytimes.com/2014/06/12/us/dave-brat-was-aided-by-laura-ingraham.html.

Powell, Larry, and Joseph Cowart. 2003. *Political Campaign Communication: Inside and Out*. Boston: Allyn and Bacon.

Sabato, Larry. 1993. *Feeding Frenzy: How Attack Journalism Has Transformed American Politics*. New York: The Free Press.

Semiatin, Richard J. 2004. *Campaigns in the 21st Century*. Boston: McGraw Hill.

Shaw, Catherine. 2014. *The Campaign Manager: Running and Winning Local Elections*, 5th edition. Boulder, CO: Westview Press.

Sides, John, DaronShaw, Matt Grossmann, and Keena Lipsitz. 2014. *Campaigns & Elections: Rules, Reality, Strategy, Choice*. New York: W.W. Norton.

4

PAID MEDIA

Advertising is where campaigns spend most of the money they raise. A typical Congressional campaign spends at least 60 percent of its budget on television ads alone. Most campaign professionals assume ads are worth the investment, but the high price tag invites skepticism. Some experts question whether campaign ads actually sway voters. This chapter will examine this question by reviewing the mechanics of campaign advertising and the scholarly research on its effectiveness.

The numbers can be staggering. During the 2014 U.S. Senate contest between incumbent Kay Hagan and her Republican challenger Thom Tillis, nearly 70,000 television ads were run between September 1 and Election Day at a total cost of $52.6 million. That same year, $9.1 million was spent on television advertising for a single race for Georgia's 12th Congressional district. In both races, the incumbent candidates lost despite outspending their opponents on the air (Fowler and Ridout 2014).

Why do campaigns spend so much on advertising when the results are often so mixed? Part of the explanation lies in the fact that, unlike with earned media, paid media gives maximum control over the content and timing of the message. A candidate can prepare for and tightly manage a press conference, but news outlets control how the event gets covered. With a TV spot, a campaign gets 30 seconds or more to communicate directly with viewers. That seems like a short amount of time, but media professionals can pack a lot in. A single 30-second spot can be used to introduce a candidate to potential voters by focusing on a few key aspects of her biography: her family, for example, along with an overview of her relevant experience. Another ad can be used to summarize the candidate's policy platform, or describe a position on a key issue. Half a minute is enough time to attack the candidate's opponent, sometimes with time to spare to briefly describe how the two candidates are different. These messages are enhanced with eye-catching visuals, music, narration and text.

As we will see, there is some evidence that campaign ads can actually do what they are designed to do: persuade voters and sometimes mobilize them to act. Political commercials also can be surprisingly informative. Before turning to their effects, however, we will review some of the fundamentals of campaign advertising.

Targeting

Targeting is a key concept in paid media. In campaigning, targeting can be defined as *communication strategies and practices aimed at focusing precious resources on particular voters or groups of voters*. Because advertising is so expensive, campaigns are motivated to deliver appropriate messages to the right people. Ideally, ads aimed at persuading people are targeted toward likely voters who have not made up their minds. An ad touting a candidate's position on gun rights should be targeted toward people who care about the issue and are likely to agree with the candidate. Pro-choice voters should be on the receiving end of messages advertising a candidate's position on abortion.

There are at least two types of targeting: *macrotargeting* and *microtargeting*. Advertising strategies are much more conducive to macrotargeting—targeting based on the aggregate characteristics of a group of people (such as the audience for a particular media outlet or program). For example, a candidate running for the Republican nomination can reach likely GOP primary voters by advertising on a conservative talk radio program. Not everyone who listens to the program is conservative, and not all of them will vote in the primaries. In other words, there is some waste. But the campaign can assume that most members of the audience lean to the right and are politically active—otherwise, why would they bother listening to a show focused on politics in which the prevailing viewpoint is conservative.

Even non-political media outlets are conducive to macrotargeting. To firm up support among conservatives, the 2004 campaign to reelect George W. Bush bought spots on the Golf Channel once it determined that the network's audience was disproportionally Republican (Ridout et al. 2012). It also invested heavily in advertising during the Summer Olympics, apparently to divert attention away from the just-completed Democratic convention. The 2004 Kerry campaign targeted programs with large African-American audiences as well as daytime and late-night talk shows (Ridout et al. 2012).

Microtargeting is more precise than macrotargeting because it is based on the known or assumed characteristics of an individual person rather than groups of individuals. If an individual belongs to the Sierra Club, a pro-environment candidate can target that individual with messages about the candidate's record on relevant issues. (Likewise, a candidate who is skeptical about climate change might avoid this voter altogether.) Campaigns cannot use television or radio to microtarget because they cannot verify that particular individuals are watching specific programs at a specific time. As we will see, this is one reason that digital and mobile ads are so enticing: theoretically at least, customized spots can appear on a device's browser or mobile app depending on the online behavior and likes/dislikes of the individual using the device. Because computers and mobile devices can be connected with individual persons, microtargeting is possible with digital media.

Outlets

This chapter focuses on television advertising, which is where most campaign advertising spending goes—62 percent of it, according to one estimate (Respaut and Lozada 2015). Television is where most scholars have focused their research and where the news media apply most of their scrutiny. First, though, we will turn our attention toward advertising on other media outlets: radio, newspapers, and the internet.

Radio ads do not get a lot of attention from scholars, but campaigns quietly embrace them. Campaigns like radio in part because it is less expensive than television. For example, radio ads made up 20 percent of all ads aired in the Little Rock media market during the 2002 elections but consumed only 2.5 percent of ad spending (Overby and Barth 2006). Because radio spots require only audio—no visuals—they are relatively easy to produce. This makes them conducive to "rapid response" to opponent attacks and breaking news. A campaign can produce and air a radio spot in a matter of hours.

Radio advertising also is more conducive to macrotargeting because audiences are narrowly defined based on the format of the station rather than the characteristics of a particular program. Campaigns can reach out to Latino voters with ads on Spanish-language radio. Ads customized for older African-American voters can be aired on stations that follow an "urban adult contemporary" format. Conservatives who vote regularly can be reached on stations that specialize in political talk radio. With radio, loyalty is high: people tend to stick with one or two stations, changing channels far less often they do with a TV remote control (Overby and Barth 2006). Listeners who tune in at home or at work sometimes keep the radio on the same station for hours at a time. If a political commercial comes on the air, audience members are likely to hear it.

Campaigns also like radio ads because they run below the radar, rarely attracting scrutiny by the news media for their truthfulness or inflammatory messaging. As a result, campaigns sometimes save their more aggressive attacks for radio. That is in part "because there is no visual connection with a candidate and less chance of a backlash against the sponsor of such an ad" (Jasperson 2005: 275). Although campaigns routinely monitor each other's paid media in case they need to respond, the sheer volume of radio ads can be overwhelming for both sides.

Newspapers. Spending on newspaper advertising is dwarfed by ads on the airwaves, but print offers key advantages over television and radio spots. Regular newspaper readers tend to vote at high rates (Edmonds 2012). Campaign ads published in local newspapers also may be perceived as more reliable and less annoying than broadcast spots (Newspaper Association of America 2012). As with radio, newspapers ads are relatively easy to produce, allowing for a quick turnaround. In addition, each media market is usually monopolized by a single local newspaper whereas multiple stations compete for the market's television viewers. Thus, a single newspaper ad might actually reach more likely voters than a spot aired on one of the local television stations. In addition, whereas television stations often run out of airtime during peak campaign season, "ad space is almost always available" in local newspapers (Burton and Shea 2010: 172). Finally, macrotargeting is possible as publishers have shifted toward geographic variation in content whereby readers receive a different edition depending on which suburban area they live in (Burton and Shea 2010).

Print ads can be advantageous for complex messages that would be difficult to convey in a 30-second spot. There is plenty of room for explanatory text. Multiple newspaper ads can be combined to tell a complicated story or explain an idea. For example, U.S. Senator Lisa Murkowski's 2004 reelection bid got a boost from a series of newspaper ads arguing that voting for Murkowski would help her home state. How? By helping Republicans keep the Senate, which would preserve the powerful influence of Ted Stevens, Alaska's senior senator. In other words, a vote for Murkowski was a vote for GOP control of the Senate, which would help Alaska because Stevens would remain in the majority. That is a difficult argument to make in a 30-second television spot (Helliker 2007).

Online digital advertising makes up a small but growing portion of campaign spending. Early in the 2012 campaign—before the air wars began on television—the Obama campaign spent more money on internet advertising than radio and television combined (Farnam 2012). According to one estimate, spending on online political ads was expected to quadruple between 2014 and 2016, surpassing newspaper ad expenditures (Respaut and Lozada 2015).

Digital media is enticing for a number of reasons. Whereas the other outlets are limited to macrotargeting, microtargeting is possible with digital media. Here is how it works. When you visit a website or buy a product online, a digital tracker is stored on your computer or device. This material is combined with other information collected about you such as the car you drive, the brands you prefer, the movies you like, the magazines you subscribe to, and your charitable contributions. Combined, these data points create an anonymous profile that guesses your demographic characteristics, political leanings, and the likelihood that you will vote in the next election (Vega 2012). If you are a regular at Chick-fil-A, drink bourbon, and drive a Land Rover, you are more likely to be a Republican. Democrats are more likely to eat at Popeyes, drink Cognac, and drive a Subaru. Church's Chicken regulars lean Democratic, but vote at low rates. Viewers of the CMT network tend to vote GOP, but vote at lower rates than other Republicans (Edsall 2012). These guesses can be wrong, but campaigns are aware of the risks and use them to target appropriate ads based on the profile that emerges (Ridout et al. 2012).

Online ads can be targeted to people who search for certain names or words. In 2012, users who Googled "immigration reform" saw an ad for the Obama campaign next to their results. Ditto for Google searches of "Warren Buffett," "Obama singing" and "Obama birthday." Rick Santorum's 2012 Republican nomination campaign bought space next to searches for "Rush Limbaugh," the conservative talk radio host (Farnam 2012). When Chris Christie ran for governor of New Jersey in 2009, his opponent attacked him for supporting cuts to health insurance coverage of mammogram testing. The Christie campaign responded with an online ad showing Christie relating his mother's struggle with breast cancer. Who saw the ad? Individuals identified as Republican women who had searched online for information about breast cancer (Vega 2012).

Mobile devices and their GPS technology enable microtargeted advertising based on where the user is at any given moment. In 2010, smartphone users attending the Minnesota State Fair received an ad from Michelle Bachmann's congressional campaign telling them that "while you're at the fair, you should know that [my opponent] voted to raise taxes on your corn dog and your deep-fried bacon and your beer" (West 2014: 8). College students helped Tom Perriello ride Obama's coattails to victory in Virginia's 5th Congressional district in 2008. Running for reelection two years later, his campaign targeted mobile phone users within three miles of the University of Virginia campus with an ad telling them how they could get a ride to the polls (Schultheis 2011).

Digital ads also are attractive due to their high "action rate." Whereas watching TV and listening to the radio is a passive activity, people interact with their digital devices. Users who click on a campaign ad may be sent to the campaign's website. There, they will be urged to provide their contact information, including their email address—invaluable information to campaigns eager to gather data about prospective voters and follow-up with appeals to contribute money, volunteer, and cast their vote.

The problem with digital is that, although it is less expensive than television, it is not exactly cheap. "Campaigns may spend between $2 and $10 (or more) per qualified supporter attracted through online ad buys" (Turk 2013: 53). That adds up quickly in a big race, and it is difficult to anticipate and therefore budget for the number of digitally acquired supporters or donors. What is more, the mechanics of targeting online ads are harder than it sounds. There is no guarantee that past web browsing behavior accurately reveals accurate information about the individual using the computer when the ad pops up. It can be difficult to connect this online data with individuals' offline profile—their likes and dislikes, the car they drive, the magazines they subscribe to, much less their partisanship and past voting behavior. That information can be obtained, but linking it to online indicators can be challenging.

Thus it should come as no surprise that digital ad spending is still dwarfed by other campaign expenditures. In 2014, candidates in the 10 most competitive House races spent more on polling and direct mail than digital advertising (Willis 2015). Old-fashioned television is still king, as we will see in the next section.

Television spots remain the dominant mode of campaign advertising. They consume as much as 75 percent of a campaign's budget. Candidates are willing to spend this much because, according to conventional wisdom, television is where campaigns go to reach "persuadables"—that is, voters who either have not made up their minds or are susceptible to change. The percentage of persuadables in the electorate can be quite small: five percent during the closing days of a high-profile election; much higher for down-ballot races early in the campaign. But a slight edge even among a fraction of one percent of the electorate can result in victory. TV remains remarkably resilient. Although a growing number of younger people are forgoing live television in favor of online programming on their laptops or tablets, older citizens still watch TV on a regular basis. Many of them are persuadable, and most of them vote.

The duration of a typical campaign spot is 30 seconds. That is not a lot of time to communicate complex political information to potential supporters. Ads are enlisted to cram in a lot of material: video, still photos, text, and narration. As a result, political spots can be simplistic and crude. But as campaigning becomes more professionalized and media-savvy, some campaigns have got creative.

U.S. Senate candidate Jodi Ernst caught a lot of flak for a 2014 ad linking her childhood on a farm castrating pigs to cutting pork-barrel spending in Washington—"Let's make 'em squeal," she said, referring to the "big spenders" in Washington while a pig literally squeals in the background. The ad may have been corny, but it conveyed Ernst's priority of cutting federal spending, and the imagery and sound effects resonated with voters in Iowa, where pig farming is a major industry. When Congressman Randy Neugebauer first ran for reelection in 2004, few people could pronounce his name. (The correct pronunciation is naw-guh-bow-er). The campaign poked fun at the problem with a television ad set in a barbershop. An elderly customer repeatedly mispronounces his name ("knock-en-power" is one example), but is patiently corrected by his younger counterparts. By the end of the 30-second spot, viewers heard six different people correctly pronounce Neugebauer's name a total of ten times. The repetition is part of the joke, making it less annoying than it could be. Farouk Shami also faced a name-related problem when he ran for the Democratic nomination to be governor of Texas. Needless to say, there are not many Texans named Farouk Shami. An immigrant from Palestine, he spoke with an accent and had never run for political office. To introduce him to Texas voters, his media consultants developed a series of ads linking Shami's story of "coming to America with $71 in his pocket to build a multibillion-dollar company with the story of Texas itself" (Devine 2013: 42). Rather than have the candidate narrate the ad, they hired someone who spoke with a Texas accent.

All of these are examples of positive ads. In truth, TV ads vary widely in terms of emphasis, tone and type. Political scientist Amy Jasperson (2005) categorizes campaign spots along three dimensions: (1) issue v. image (2) positive v. negative v. comparative and (3) attack v. counterattack v. inoculation. In the first dimension, *issue* ads center on one or more of the candidate's or opponent's policy positions whereas *image* ads focus on biography, personality or leadership style. In the second, positive spots focus on the favorable attributes of the candidate sponsoring the ad whereas negative ads mostly criticize the opponent. Comparative spots—sometimes called contrast ads—contain messages about both candidates, positive for the sponsor and negative for the opponent. The third dimension distinguishes between ads attacking a candidate, counterattack ads aimed at responding to the original attack, and spots that attempt to inoculate a candidate against an attack before it happens.

Negativity

The majority of ads are mostly negative, even comparative spots that contain at least some positive information about the ad's sponsor. In presidential elections, negative messages have prevailed on television since 1964, when the Lyndon Johnson campaign ran a serious of ads attacking Barry Goldwater, including the infamous "Daisy" spot. Negative advertising dipped sharply in 1972 and 1976, perhaps due to backlash following the escalation of attacks in the previous two elections. But negativity rebounded in subsequent elections, peaking in 1988, when negative ads made up more than 80 percent of prominent presidential campaign ads. Since then, roughly two-thirds of prominent presidential campaign ads have been negative overall (West 2014). In 2008, the Obama campaign was so flush with cash that it could afford to spend more than usual on positive spots—including a 30-minute infomercial that ran during prime time. His opponent John McCain was relatively low on funds and behind for most of the race; 79 percent of his ads were negative (West 2014). In 2014, just over 50 percent of ads aired in congressional races were negative compared with 23 percent comparative and 26 percent positive. That is a bit less negative than in 2010, when 55% of ads were negative. Why the slight decline? Apparently some pro-GOP independent groups were experimenting with airing positive ads (Fowler and Ridout 2014).

Darrell West, author of the seminal *Air Wars* (2014), specifies four principles used by strategists to influence voters—all of them prominent in negative advertising. Ad strategists employ these principles because a campaign spot must pack a lot of messaging into a 30-second spot. Shortcuts are necessary. One, many ads rely on *stereotypes* about the two parties. An ad that builds on the stereotype that Republicans are anti-gay can resonate just as effectively as ads portraying a Democratic candidate as anti-religion. Two, ads can use *association* to link a candidate with an unpopular person or idea. In 2008, for example, many Obama spots associated John McCain with President Bush, some featuring a famous photo of McCain and Bush embracing. Two years later, Republican candidates used imagery to associate their Democratic opponents with a then-unpopular President Obama. Three, ads can *demonize* an opponent by portraying them as an evil, extreme, immoral, or destructive character. Combined with the association principle, demonization has been used to equate a candidate's policy record with such evildoers as Adolph Hitler and Osama bin Laden. Four, ads can use *code words* that play on negative stereotypes about the two parties. A Republican might be described as a "right-wing extremist," a Democrat as a "ultra-liberal" or "socialist." With all of these principles, there must be a kernel of truth to these messages to be effective. Although these appeals are often misleading or exaggerated, "[t]here must be some believability in the specific appeal for an ad to have credibility" (West 2014: 14).

Producing and Buying Time

Most campaign spots are produced by paid media consultants hired by the campaigns. Ad production is much faster today due to digital technology. "An ad can go from concept to execution, to delivery, to broadcast, all in the same day" (Devine 2013: 36).

Opposition research is crucial to the production of negative ads. "Oppo" is the investigation of an opponent's political and personal record. The investigation might reveal controversial legislative votes, policy failures, personal scandals, health problems, financial struggles, and anything else that a campaign might use against its opponent. In a political ad, the fruits of oppo appear in the form of specific references to an opponent's support for unpopular legislation; direct quotes from a critical news report or editorial; or a video clip of the opposing candidate committing a gaffe. Two of these elements appeared in a 2014 ad attacking Connecticut gubernatorial candidate Tom Foley. The ad features a video clip of Foley seemingly blaming workers for the closure of a paper goods plant, telling them "You have failed, because you have lost these jobs." It also cites the *Hartford Courant* to back up its claim that Foley benefited financially by forcing a company into bankruptcy.

A typical campaign spot combines video, still photos, quotes, and voice-over narration. It also must squeeze in a disclaimer. By law, candidates for federal office must "stand by their ad"—that is, record a statement affirming that they approve of the ad's message. A provision of the Bipartisan Campaign Reform Act of 2002, the requirement is aimed at discouraging candidates from making unfair attacks. Candidates usually say something like "I am Barack Obama, and I approve this message." The statement typically appears at the end and can consume four to six precious seconds of airtime. In one ad, Senator Rand Paul injected political messaging to his disclaimer when he said, "I'm Rand Paul, and I approve of this message because government is the servant, not the master" (Devine 2013: 32).

Media consultants also take the lead on buying air time, otherwise known as ad buys. "The heart of a candidate's advertising strategy concerns decisions on when, where and how often to broadcast ads" (West 2014: 29).

When? Certain types of ads work best at certain stages of the campaign. Early in the race, candidate's use their ads to define themselves—and their opponents. Traditionally this is done through positive biographical or "establishment" spots. For unfamiliar candidates, establishment ads briefly introduce voters to key biographical assets and policy priorities. For well-known candidates, the objective is to remind voters of the candidate's most positive qualities.

Negative ads also are common during this stage as candidates attempt to define their opponent before the opponent can define her or himself. Early in the 2012 campaign, the Obama campaign ran attack spots to define Mitt Romney as an out-of-touch plutocrat. Obama's "Makes You Wonder" ad raised questions about Romney's unwillingness to make his tax returns public. Another ad featured footage of Romney's awkward, off-key singing of "America the Beautiful" as a backdrop to news headlines such as "As Governor, Romney Outsourced Jobs to India" and "In business, Mitt Romney's firms shipped jobs to Mexico." Both ads ran between the Republican primaries and the party conventions, well before Romney could re-introduce himself to the general electorate.

Buying early also can help the campaign save money. In competitive races, the best discounted time slots get snatched up months in advance. In 2012, Romney bought late and paid more as a result. His campaign opted to book commercials on a week-to-week basis rather than months in advance. This approach gave the campaign more flexibility, but it resulted in higher rates and sometimes lower reach. "In some states such as Iowa, Ohio, and Wisconsin, Republicans outspent Democrats by three to two but reached fewer people" (West 2014: 33).

Even so, campaigns often save their ad buys for the end of the race. Bill Clinton's 1992 campaign saved its big ad buys for the final two weeks of the campaign (West 2014). Until then, many uncommitted voters are not paying close attention. And because the effects of campaign ads can be so short-lived, under-financed campaigns may be better served holding off until the final weeks of the election (Hill et al. 2013: 542).

Where? Campaigns buy time on both broadcast and cable stations. Cable is attractive partly because it is more conducive to macrotargeting (see page 64). The 2004 George W. Bush campaign bought time on the Golf Channel because they were so many conservative males in the audience. In 2012, Obama invested heavily in cable advertising for the sake of cost efficiency. Cable companies also may serve smaller markets more efficiently than some of their broadcast competitors. "Local cable companies have fixed, identifiable borders, and these boundaries might be contiguous, or roughly so, with electoral districts" (Burton and Shea 2010: 170).

That said, broadcast outlets continue to attract the lion's share of spending: over 50 percent of campaign ad expenditures goes toward broadcast television compared with 10 percent for cable (Respaut and Lozada 2015). For all the talk of declining audiences, broadcast networks still garner higher ratings than cable. Broadcast networks' resilience also stems from discounted ad rates. Under Federal Communication Commission regulations, broadcast television and radio stations must offer candidates a discounted rate—specifically, the lowest rate charged by the station for a comparable time slot. The discount applies to ads run 45 days before a primary or caucus and 60 days prior to a general election or runoff. The problem is that discounted prime-time slots sometimes sell out during competitive races. When that happens, campaigns are stuck paying top dollar for last-minute purchases.

The evening news is the most obvious program during which to run political ads. News watchers tend to be politically engaged and likely to vote. In 2008, 50 percent of all presidential campaign ads ran during news programs (Ridout et al. 2012). The Obama campaign focused its ad buys on local news outlets rather than the national network programs because of high viewership among persuadable voters (Plouffe 2009). "Going local" rather than national also allows presidential campaigns to focus resources on battleground states. Because ads run on local media get less scrutiny from national news outlets, presidential campaigns sometimes "hide" attack ads through local buys and save their positive spots for national media.

How often? Voters get tired of seeing the same ads over and over again. Campaigns must weigh the pros of repetition versus the cons of overexposure and voter fatigue. In 1992, President George H.W. Bush's campaign favored repletion over variety by spreading nine ads across the entire fall campaign whereas Ross Perot ran 29 different spots and Clinton ran 17 (West 2014).

Of course, high costs keep campaigns from running more ads than they do. Much depends on where the candidate is running. Some markets are more expensive and less cost-efficient than others. To reach voters in many of Virginia's Congressional districts, campaigns must buy ads in the entire Greater Washington media market. That means ads aimed at voters in the desired Virginia district also reach viewers in Maryland and the District of Columbia, as well as those in other Congressional districts in the state. Statewide races in New Jersey are notoriously wasteful because campaigns must run ads in both the New York and Philadelphia media markets, which means the ads are reaching viewers in those states as well as adjoining Delaware, which gets most of its broadcast TV from the Philadelphia stations.

Costs vary depending on what media professionals call reach and frequency (Burton and Shea 2010: 162–163). Reach is the share of targeted voters who see the ad. Frequency is the number of times a voter is reached. The combined measurement of these two concepts is called gross rating points (GRP), which is calculated by multiplying reach times frequency. So, if an ad is played twice during a program that claims 10 percent reach, then the GRP is 20. In truth, more so than these metrics, campaigns are more interested in the "cost to reach voters who are persuadable" (Burton and Shea 2010: 163). Everything else is waste.

Ads as Earned Media

Campaign advertising can make news. News coverage of ads can take a number of forms. As part of their watchdog role, news outlets scrutinize the accuracy of campaign ads through what are called "ad watches"—in-depth assessments of the accuracy of campaign spots. (See Box 4.1 below). If an ad is controversial, media outlets will cover it just like they would any other campaign flap. Sometimes this results in unwanted scrutiny. That happened to U.S. Senator Mark Begich when his 2014 reelection campaign ran an ad attacking his opponent's position on punishing sex offenders by referencing a horrific crime murder of an elderly couple and sex assault of their two-year-old granddaughter. News coverage was harsh, and the Begich campaign eventually pulled the ad after initially refusing to do so.

BOX 4.1 SPOT CHECKS

Ad watches are where paid and earned media intersect. One advantage of paid media is that the campaign has almost complete control over the message—no pesky reporters to wrestle with. But sometimes news outlets and watchdog groups muddy the campaign's message by scrutinizing the veracity of its ads. Also known as fact checks, ad watches are reports that dissect a specific spot and evaluate its accuracy, sometimes providing a rating.

For example, *The Washington Post*'s Fact Checker column rates political statements and campaign ads on a scale of one to four "Pinocchios." A spot gets one Pinocchio if it merely shades the facts, selectively tells the truth, and provides "some omissions and exaggerations, but no outright falsehoods." Four Pinocchios go to "whoppers." The *Tampa Bay Times'* PolitiFact website uses a Truth-o-Meter scale, rating statements on a scale of "true" and "mostly true" to "false," "mostly false" and in some cases, "pants on fire!" for wholly inaccurate, ridiculous claims. A 2014 ad by NARAL Pro-Choice America got a "pants on fire!" rating for implying that Republican Cory Gardner would support banning condoms if elected to the U.S. Senate. A National Rifle Association ad got the same rating for an ad attacking Democratic Senator Mary Landrieu for voting to "take away your gun rights" when all she did was vote to confirm Sonia Sotomayor to the Supreme Court five years earlier.

Ad watches grew in popularity in the wake of the 1988 presidential election, when the news media were criticized for failing to scrutinize unfair and inaccurate attacks. They exploded in 2012—"the most fact checked election in history," observed David Carr, media critic for *The New York Times* (quoted in Fridkin, Kenney and Wintersieck 2015: 128). By then, fact checking by television and print news outlets had been joined by watchdog groups such as FactCheck.org, a project of the Annenberg Public Policy Center of the University of Pennsylvania.

Do they work? How effective are ad watches at setting the record straight? Critics point out that when a TV spot is scrutinized on television, the ad is aired for free. Viewers are exposed to the ad's message and may even miss the report's critical tone. Early research on ad watches showed that ad watches may actually backfire, helping the inaccurate ad's sponsor rather than diminishing its credibility (Ansolabehere and Iyengar 1995; McKinnon and Kaid 1999). But ad watches and fact checking have since become more rigorous and recent studies suggest that they work as intended. Especially when they challenge the truthfulness of a negative ad, they shape people's assessments of the spot's accuracy, usefulness, and tone, diminishing the likelihood that the ad's claims will be accepted (Fridkin, Kenney and Wintersieck 2015). Ads deemed inaccurate may actually decrease the likelihood that audience members will vote for their sponsor (Min 2002).

But campaigns sometimes benefit from the media's interest in an "ad controversy" story. In 1996, the Republican National Committee ran an ad attacking President Clinton for legal maneuvers to postpone a sexual harassment case until after he left office. "This ad attracted front-page coverage across the nation" (Iyengar 2011: 2), presumably helping the Republicans. Perhaps the earliest example is the infamous Daisy ad produced by the Johnson campaign during the 1964 election. The ad depicted a little girl in a meadow plucking petals from a daisy while slowly counting to ten. After she says "9," she is interrupted by an adult male voice who recites an ominous countdown. At zero, a mushroom cloud fills the screen accompanied by a loud explosion. The ad closes with the message, "Vote for President Johnson on November 3." Clearly the Johnson campaign was inviting the inference that electing his opponent Barry Goldwater might result in a nuclear war. The ad aired only once, but it was shown in its entirety in news stories on the ABC and CBS Evening News. "The LBJ campaign agreed to 'pull' the ad in response to a criticism from a variety of sources, but their point about Goldwater and the risks of nuclear war had already reached the vast majority of the electorate" (Iyengar 2011: 3).

In 2004, John Kerry's Vietnam War record was attacked in a series of ads sponsored by the Swift Boat Veterans for Truth, an outside group. The group paid to run the ad in a small number of media markets, but the ads made national news for days. According to one poll, "nearly two-thirds of voters said they had heard of the Swift Boat ads," making it "one of the most successful small ad buys in the history of American campaigns" (West 2014: 33)

Sometimes campaigns engage in *phantom* or *vapor* ad buys whereby the spot is released to the media, posted online, but only minimally aired on television (or not at all). The hope is that voters will see the ad in a news story, eliminating the need to pay to run the spot on the air. Journalists complain that such ads amount to video news releases pretending to be paid advertising (West 2014). But the strategy often works. In 2011, the Democratic National Committee spent a paltry $21,930 to run an ad ridiculing Mitt Romney for flip-flopping on abortion and health care. It only ran a few times, but the ad drew heavy news coverage from a wide variety of media outlets. The fact that more than a third of the ad buy went to the cable channels in DC—where many journalists live—conveyed the impression that the buy was bigger than it was (Cillizza 2011).

Effectiveness

Do campaign ads work? In other words, are voters influenced by the ads in ways the sponsors intended? The evidence is mixed—not exactly reassuring given all the money being spent. But there is plenty of research showing that political ads can be impactful even in competitive, ad-saturated elections.

One area of research examines how much voters learn from political ads. Here the evidence is encouraging. In one study of the 2000 presidential and congressional elections, campaigns ad exposure produced modest but significant improvements in citizens' level of interest in the election, knowledge about the candidates, and likelihood of voting (Freedman, Franz, and Goldstein 2004). Other studies also show that campaign ads can be quite informative (Zhao and Chaffee 1995; Valentino, Hutchings and Williams 2004)—even more so than television news (Patterson and McClure 1976; Brians and Wattenberg 1996) and, by some measures, candidate debates (Just, Crigler and Wallach 1990).

How could that be? After all, most campaign ads are 30 seconds in length. They can be misleading, clichéd and downright silly. Part of the explanation lies in the policy-based content of typical campaign spots. Whereas news stories tend to focus on who is ahead and who is behind (see Chapter 1), 90 percent of general election campaign ads contain some policy-related information (Freedman, Franz, and Goldstein 2004). Indeed:

> Campaign ads tend to be rich in informational content, and advertising conveys information in an efficient, easily digestible way. Like product advertising, political commercials are carefully tested and skillfully produced. Text, image, and music work to complement and reinforce each other. And an ad's basic message—its bottom line—is usually simply to identify.
>
> *(Freedman, Franz, and Goldstein 2004: 725)*

In other words, campaign ads are like "multivitamins: attractively (and expertly) packaged, simple to comprehend, easy to digest" (Freedman, Franz, and Goldstein 2004: 726).

In one study, informational and mobilization effects were concentrated among citizens with relatively low levels of preexisting political knowledge (Freedman, Franz, and Goldstein 2004). Campaigns strategists know that these citizens are more likely to be up for grabs—i.e., persuadable—than highly informed likely voters. The people who have not made up their minds late in the race tend to be less informed, less engaged citizens who may or may not show up on Election Day. Most campaign ads are designed to get these citizens to make up their minds in a way that is favorable to the ad's sponsors.

Can they? How effective are campaign ads at *persuading* voters to vote for the candidate who sponsored the ad? Under John Zaller's (1992) seminal receive–accept–sample (RAS) theory, persuasion requires that individuals both *receive* and *accept* the message. As the above study reminds us, the more politically aware people are, they more likely they are to *receive* campaign messages. Politically aware citizens follow the news, show interest in politics, talk politics with others, and pay attention when they see a campaign ad. But these same individuals also tend to have strong party identification and therefore are less likely to *accept* a message that runs counter to their existing views. Likewise, less politically aware citizens tend to be up for grabs—i.e., more likely to *accept* the message—yet they are less likely to *receive* the message in the first place because they rarely seek out political information and often simply tune it out. The challenge for campaigns is that their ads are aimed at persuading citizens who have not made up their minds, yet these persuadable citizens are hard to reach. Experimental evidence suggests that campaign ads are capable of persuading individuals with low levels of political awareness (Valentino, Hutchings and Williams 2004). Less clear is whether these individuals watch campaign ads in the real world.

One reason it is difficult to isolate the persuasion effects of ads is because there are so many other potential sources of influence: news coverage, campaign events such as debates, and fieldwork. One innovative study of presidential election advertising in 2004 partly solved this problem by focusing on respondents who live in non-contested states that adjoin battleground states. Delaware, for example, is a reliable Democratic state, which means neither party spends much time or resources there on fieldwork, candidate appearances, or campaign events. But Delaware is located in the Philadelphia-area media market, and Pennsylvania was a battleground state in 2004. That meant Delaware voters were exposed to millions of dollars in campaign ads intended for Pennsylvania voters—and not much else. Thus, when the researchers found that voters in states like Delaware were impacted by campaign messages, they could more confidently attribute the attitude change to the ads since other sources of influence were minimized (Huber and Arceneaux 2007).

This study found evidence of persuasion effects—specifically, that ads partly caused citizens to shift their preferences toward the candidate who sponsored the ad. Other studies also have found evidence of ad-induced persuasion. In 1996, for example, advertising had a persuasive effect on individual voting behavior in various U.S. Senate races (Goldstein and Freedman 2000). Ditto for the 2000 presidential race between Al Gore and George W. Bush (Valentino, Hutchings and Williams 2004), and the 2008 campaign between Barack Obama and John McCain (Franz and Ridout 2010). At least one study suggests that for relatively unknown candidates, positive ads can create favorable first impressions and blunt the impact of an opponent's attack (Kahn and Geer 1994).

For campaigns, one problem is that even when ad-induced effects occur, they can be short-lived, sometimes decaying within days of exposure (Gerber et al. 2011; Hill et al. 2013; Sides and Vavreck 2013). The decay can be pronounced among supporters of the candidate being attacked by the ad, who are naturally inclined to counter-argue with the ad's message until its initial persuasion effect dissipates (Bartels 2014). For less resourced campaigns, the best strategy may be to "save their limited funds to match or exceed their opponents at the end of the race, even if this means allowing their opponents to dominate earlier advertising" (Hill et al. 2013: 542). Ad-induced persuasion effects can last for weeks among undecided voters (Bartels 2014)—long enough to be decisive in the final weeks of a tight race.

Interestingly, ads may be most impactful in low-profile Congressional and local races in which voters have weaker existing preferences (Jasperson 2005). Presidential and competitive Senate and gubernatorial races are often saturated with equal amounts of television advertising from both sides, resulting in a cancelling effect. That certainly was the case in 2012, when voters in battle-ground states were inundated with both Obama and Romney ads (Sides and Vavreck 2013).

Sometimes, though, one side outspends the other on the airwaves. This can happen even in presidential elections. In 2004, pro-Kerry ads outnumbered pro-Bush ads by a roughly three-to-two margin. Most of the pro-Kerry ads were sponsored by outside groups, and because federal law prohibits such groups from coordinating their efforts with the campaigns, Kerry's ad advantage may have been mitigated by inconsistent messages and overlapping ad buys. Anyway, Kerry lost. But one study suggests that Kerry's overall ad advantage may have helped him narrow the gap a bit (Franz and Ridout 2010). In 2008, Obama ads out-numbered McCain ads by more than 40 percent. Because Obama raised so much more money than McCain, nearly all of his ads were sponsored by the campaign whereas McCain had to rely on the Republican Party and outside groups. Obama won by a larger margin than can be explained by his ad advantage. But according to one study, had his campaign purchased only 75 percent of the ads it bought in October, Obama might have lost more than 300,000 votes nationwide as well as North Carolina, Florida and perhaps Indiana in the Electoral College (Franz and Ridout 2010).

In short, there is enough evidence of persuasion and other effects that campaigns feel compelled to spend thousands and sometimes millions to run ads on television. Getting outspent on the airwaves can result in a loss of a percentage point or two, and that can be decisive in a tight race. Campaigns are risk averse. When they can afford it, they will opt to spend more money than necessary on television despite knowing that their ads may be merely counterbalancing ad expenditures by their opponent.

Issue ads by outside groups

Campaigns are not the only source of political ads. Political parties and independent groups have been airing so-called "issue ads" since the beginning of modern campaign finance law. By the mid-1990s, parties and groups had identified a loophole in campaign finance law that allowed them to spend unlimited funds on advertising as long as they focused on policy issues rather than explicitly advocating for the election or defeat of a particular candidate. That simply meant avoiding words and phrases such as "vote for," "vote against," "elect," "defeat," "reject," and "cast your ballot for." In every other way, though, these ads looked and sounded like standard campaign spots. The fact that they ran during campaign season belied the notion that these were anything but campaign ads. That is certainly what they looked and sounded like to voters.

The 2002 Bipartisan Campaign Reform Act (BCRA) was supposed to close this loophole. But in 2010, the Supreme Court ruled much of BCRA unconstitutional in its landmark *Citizens United v. Federal Election Commission* decision. Among other things, *Citizens United* ruled that the government could not effectively distinguish between campaigning and other forms of political advocacy. More importantly, it ruled that the First Amendment prohibited the government from restricting independent political spending by non-profit groups, corporations, and labor unions. Outside groups were now free to raise and spend as much money as they could on campaign ads.

Independent, non-candidate-sponsored ads have since exploded. In many of the most competitive Senate races in 2014, outside groups ran more TV ads than the political parties and—in some cases—the candidates' campaigns (Fowler and Ridout 2014). In Michigan's Senate race that year, 53.1 percent of TV ads aired between January 1 to Election Day were sponsored by outside groups (Fowler and Ridout 2014). During the 2012 Republican presidential nomination campaign, the majority of ads were run by "Super PACs"—outside groups created to take advantage of the new deregulated environment. Most of the ads were negative (West 2014).

Initially, Super PACs attracted the most scrutiny from reformers because the amounts were so staggering and their ads were so overwhelmingly negative. Most recently, "dark money" spending by non-profit organizations has raised further alarm. Unlike Super PACs, non-profits are not required to disclose their donors. TV ad spending by these groups made up about 35 percent of overall TV ad expenditures in House, Senate, and Gubernatorial elections in 2014. More than half of TV ad spending on the Republican side was made by dark-money groups (Fowler and Ridout 2014).

What is the big deal? After all, federal law prohibits groups from directly coordinating their efforts with the campaigns. The groups are supposed to be wholly independent. Yet critics raise a number of concerns. One stems from confusion over what separates the candidates' campaigns from the independent groups that support them. The Federal Election Commission—the agency charged with regulating campaign fundraising and spending for federal elections—prohibits a campaign from coordinating its paid communication with outside groups. But the rules do not ban working together on other forms of communication, nor do they prevent campaigns from sharing their advertising plans. "For all practical purposes, there are no prohibitions against coordination," says Fred Wertheimer, an advocate for tighter regulations. As a result, all of the major 2016 presidential candidates had their own Super PACs. In addition to running ads, the groups provided the campaigns with ad-support services as video footage and opposition research (Gold 2015).

Another concern is that a single wealthy individual can influence elections by pouring—and sometimes hiding—huge sums of money into loosely regulated entities. Casino magnate Sheldon Adelson contributed $93 million to Super PACs during the 2012 campaign. He kept afloat Newt Gingrich's GOP nomination candidacy with $15 million in contributions to Winning Our Future, a pro-Gingrich Super PAC (Cillizza 2014). Adelson also gave directly to Gingrich's campaign, but his contribution was capped at $2,500—the legal limit for individual contributions directly to the campaigns. By contributing to a Super PAC, Adelson was allowed to multiply his donations to Gingrich by 6,000. And now with the more recent "dark money" loophole, massive contributions like this can be made without disclosing the source.

Another concern is that outside groups can more easily get away with unfair attacks. Candidates are required by law to take responsibility for the ads they sponsor. They risk backlash if an ad crosses the line in the minds of voters. But who is to blame if an unfair attack is launched by a group with an innocuous, non-partisan name like "Priorities USA" (a pro-Democratic group) or "American Crossroads" (a pro-Republican group)? An example from an earlier era illustrates the disconnect. During the 1988 presidential campaign, an outside group supporting George H.W. Bush ran a spot attacking his opponent, Massachusetts Governor Michael Dukakis, for supporting a prison furlough program that resulted in the release of convicted murderer Willie Horton, who later raped one victim and stabbed her boyfriend. Critics attacked the ad's racial overtones, but the Bush campaign was able to avoid direct responsibility despite benefiting from the attack. Similarly, President George W. Bush benefited from—but did not take responsibility for—controversial ads attacking John Kerry for his Vietnam War record. The ads were sponsored by a group called Swift Boat Veterans for Truth—an innocuous name that masked the ads' erroneous content and pro-Bush intentions. In 2012, an ad sponsored by a pro-Obama group made a spurious link between Mitt Romney's leadership of Bain Capital and the death of the wife of Joe Soptic, a worker who lost his health insurance when Bain closed the factory where he worked. The Obama campaign distanced itself from the ad, but only after the ad had been widely circulated.

According to some studies, ads sponsored by generically named, unknown independent groups may be more effective than ads sponsored by the candidates

(Brooks and Murov 2012; Ridout, Franz and Fowler 2014). That may be because voters sometimes penalize the candidate who sponsored a harsh attack ad whereas they do not know whom to blame for an ad sponsored by a vaguely named group. Thus it will surprise no one if such groups continue to "do the dirty work of running these kinds of harsh attack ads that the candidates would rather not do themselves" (Brooks and Murov 2012: 404).

Conclusion

Citizens may complain about political ads—sometimes for good reason—but professionals see them as crucial outlets for communicating with potential voters. Ads may not sway voters as much as the pros think, but not all of that money being poured into paid media is going to waste. A growing number of studies show that campaign spots can move an impressive number of voters, even if the effects fade quickly. In contrast with the perilous unpredictability of working with the news media, political ads allow campaigns to communicate directly with voters in their own words, style and format. This high level of control makes paid media worth the investment for the campaigns. But both earned and paid media suffer from significant shortcomings. In the next chapter, we will examine how campaigns are using social media to chip away at some of their limitations.

References

Ansolabehere, Stephen, and Shanto Iyengar. 1995. *Going Negative: How Political Advertisements Shrink and Polarize the Electorate*. New York: The Free Press.

Bartels, Larry M. 2014. "Remembering to Forget: A Note on the Duration of Campaign Advertising Effects." *Political Communication* 31: 532–544.

Brians, Craig Leonard, and Martin P. Wattenberg. 1996. "Campaign Issue Knowledge and Salience: Comparing Reception from TV Commercials, TV News and Newspapers." *American Journal of Political Science* 40(1): 172–193.

Brooks, Deborah Jordan, and Michael Murov. 2012. "Assessing Accountability in a Post-Citizens United Era: The Effects of Attack Ad Sponsorship by Unknown Independent Groups." *American Politics Research* 40(3): 383–418.

Burton, Michael John, and Daniel M. Shea. 2010. *Campaign Craft: The Strategies, Tactics, and Art of Political Campaign Management*, 4th edition. Santa Barbara, CA: Praeger.

Cillizza, Chris. 2014. "Sheldon Adelson spent $93 million on the 2012 election. Here's how." *The Washington Post*, March 25. http://www.washingtonpost.com/blogs/the-fix/wp/2014/03/25/sheldon-adelson-spent-93-million-on-the-2012-election-heres-how/.

Cillizza, Chris. 2011. "The DNC's Phantom Ad Buy—and Why it Worked." *The Washington Post*, Nov. 30. http://www.washingtonpost.com/blogs/the-fix/post/the-dncs-phantom-ad-buy-and-why-it-worked/2011/11/30/gIQAdhaaDO_blog.html.

Devine, Tad. 2013. "Paid Media—In an Era of Rapid and Revolutionary Change." In *Campaigns on the Cutting Edge*, 2nd edition, ed. Richard Semiatin. Los Angeles: Sage/CQ Press.

Edmonds, Tom. 2012. "Why Newspaper Advertising Still Matters." *Campaigns & Elections*, Feb. 19. http://www.campaignsandelections.com/campaign-insider/693/why-newspaper-advertising-still-matters.

Edsall, Thomas B. "Let the Nanotargeting Begin." *The New York Times*, April 15: http://campaignstops.blogs.nytimes.com/2012/04/15/let-the-nanotargeting-begin/?_r=2.

Farnam, T.W. 2012. "Obama Has Aggressive Internet Strategy to Woo Voters." *Washington Post*, April 6. http://www.washingtonpost.com/politics/obama-has-aggressive-internet-strategy-to-woo-supporters/2012/04/06/gIQAavB2zS_story.html.

Fowler, Erika Franklin, and Travis N. Ridout. 2014. "Political Advertising in 2014: The Year of the Outside Group." *The Forum* 12(4): 663–684.

Franz, Michael, and Travis N. Ridout. 2010. "Political Advertising and Persuasion in the 2004 and 2008 Presidential Elections." *American Politics Research* 38(2): 303–329.

Freedman, Paul, Michael Franz, and Kenneth Goldstein. 2004. "Campaign Advertising and Democratic Citizenship." *American Journal of Political Science* 48(4): 723–741.

Fridkin, Kim, Patrick J. Kenney, and Amanda Wintersieck. 2015. "Liar, Liar, Pants on Fire: How Fact-Checking Influences Citizens' Reactions to Negative Advertising." *Political Communication* 32: 127–151.

Gerber, Alan S., James G. Gimpel, Donald P. Green, and Daron R. Shaw. 2011. "How Large and Long-lasting Are the Persuasive Effects of Televised Campaign Ads? Results from a Randomized Field Experiment." *American Political Science Review* 105(1): 135–150.

Gold, Matea. 2015. "Super PACs' role grows ever larger." *Washington Post* (July 7): A4.

Goldstein, Ken, and Paul Freedman. 2000. "New Evidence for New Arguments: Money and Advertising in the 1996 Senate Elections." *Journal of Politics* 62(4): 1087–1108.

Helliker, Kevin. 2007. "Political Ads Stage a Comeback in Newspapers." *The Wall Street Journal*. http://www.wsj.com/articles/SB118541344062578440.

Hill, Seth J., James Lo, Lynn Vavreck, and John Zaller. 2013. "How Quickly We Forget: The Duration of Persuasion Effects from Mass Communication." *Political Communication* 30(4): 521–547.

Huber, Gregory A., and Kevin Arceneaux. 2007. "Identifying the Persuasive Effects of Presidential Advertising." *American Journal of Political Science* 51(4): 957–977.

Iyengar, Shanto. 2011. "The Media Game: New Moves, Old Strategies." *The Forum* 9(1): Article 1.

Jasperson, Amy E. 2005. "Campaign Communications." In *Guide to Political Campaigns in America*, ed. Paul S. Herrnson. Washington, DC: CQ Press.

Just, Marion, Ann Crigler, and Lori Wallach. 1990. "Thirty Seconds or Thirty Minutes: What Viewers Learned from Spot Advertisements and Candidate Debates." *Journal of Communication* 40: 120–133.

Kahn, Kim Fridkin, and John G. Geer. 1994. "Creating Impressions: An Experimental Investigation of Political Advertising on Television." *Political Behavior* 16(1): 93–116.

McKinnon, Lori Melton, and Lynda Lee Kaid. 1999. "Exposing Negative Campaigning or Enhancing Advertising Effects: An Experimental Study of Adwatch Effects on Voters' Evaluations of Candidates and Their Ads." *Journal of Applied Communication Research* 27(3): 217–236.

Min, Young. 2002. "Intertwining of Campaign News and Advertising: The Content and Electoral Effects of Newspaper Ad Watches." *Journalism & Mass Communication Quarterly* 79(4): 927–944.

Newspaper Association of America. 2012. "Readers Vote, Readers Read." http://www.naa.org/Topics-and-Tools/Advertising/Sales-Collateral/2012/readers-vote-voters-read.aspx.

Overby, Marvin L., and Jay Barth. 2006. "Radio Advertising in American Political Campaigns: The Persistence, Importance, and Effects of Narrowcasting." *American Politics Research* 34(4): 451–478.

Patterson, Thomas E., and Robert D. McClure. 1976. *The Unseeing Eye: The Myth of Television Power in National Elections.* New York: Putnam.

Plouffe, David. 2009. *The Audacity to Win: The Inside Story and Lessons of Barack Obama's Historic Victory.* New York: Viking.

Respaut, Robin, and Lucas Iberico Lozada. 2015. "'Slicing and Dicing': How Some U.S. Firms Could Win Big in 2016 Elections." *Reuters*, April 14. http://www.reuters.com/a rticle/2015/04/14/us-usa-election-data-idUSKBN0N509O20150414.

Ridout, Travis N., Michael Franz, and Erika Franklin Fowler. 2014. "Sponsorship, Disclosure, and Donors: Limiting the Impact of Outside Group Ads." *Political Research Quarterly*: 1–13.

Ridout, Travis N., Michael Franz, Kenneth M. Goldstein, and William J. Feltus. 2012. "Separation by Television Program: Understanding the Targeting of Political Advertising in Presidential Elections." *Political Communication* 29(1): 1–23.

Schultheis, Emily. 2011. "Political Advertisements Go Mobile for 2012 Elections." *Politico*, Nov. 28. http://www.politico.com/news/stories/1111/69239.html.

Sides, John, and Lynn Vavreck. 2013. *The Gamble: Choice and Chance in the 2012 Presidential Election.* Princeton, NJ: Princeton University Press.

Turk, Michael. 2013. "Social and New Media—An Evolving Future." In *Campaigns on the Cutting Edge*, 2nd edition, ed. Richard Semiatin. Los Angeles: Sage/CQ Press.

Valentino, Nicholas A., Vincent L. Hutchings, and Dmitri Williams. 2004. "The Impact of Political Advertising on Knowledge, Internet Information Seeking, and Candidate Preference." *Journal of Communication* (June): 337–354.

Vega, Tanzina. 2012. "Online Data Helping Campaigns Customize Ads." *The New York Times*, Feb. 20. http://www.nytimes.com/2012/02/21/us/politics/campaigns-use-m icrotargeting-to-attract-supporters.html?hp.

West, Darrell M. 2014. *Air Wars: Television Advertising and Social Media in Election Campaigns 1952–2012*, 6th edition. Thousand Oaks, CA: CQ Press.

Willis, Derek. 2015. "Online Political Ads Have Been Slow to Catch On as TV Reigns." *The New York Times*, Jan. 29. http://www.nytimes.com/2015/01/30/upshot/why-onli ne-political-ads-have-been-slow-to-catch-on.html?_r=0.

Zaller, John R. 1992. *The Nature and Origins of Mass Opinions.* Cambridge, MA: Cambridge University Press.

Zhao, Xinshu, and Steven H. Chaffee. 1995. "Campaign Advertisements versus Television News as Sources of Political Issue Information." *Public Opinion Quarterly* 59(1): 41–65.

5

SOCIAL MEDIA

January 2008: John McCain was back. Formerly the front runner for the Republican presidential nomination, he had stumbled badly throughout much of the early campaign. But now he was surging in the polls and the early primaries were approaching. Money was tight, however, due to profligate spending early in the campaign and lackluster fundraising. Fortunately for the campaign, one of its weapons would cost virtually nothing: "A Tale of Two Mitts," a scathing 60-second spot attacking his opponent Mitt Romney for flip-flopping on abortion, gun rights, and his fealty to the Republican Party. This was a no-frills production: mostly a few recent video clips of Romney speaking on these issues contrasted with older clips from his political career in Massachusetts. For example, a 1994 clip depicting Romney saying, "I believe abortion should be safe and legal in this country" was followed by a 2007 clip of him saying, "I am pro-life, and favor that legislation." It was a relatively lengthy ad—twice as long as the usual 30-second spot; running it on TV would have busted the campaign's depleted budget. Anyway, the low-fi production would have seemed out of place on television.

No matter: the ad was designed for online consumption, loaded onto McCain's YouTube channel. People could view it for free. Supporters could share a link to the video with their friends. Reporters could easily locate it, watch it for themselves, and cover it as a story; at least one news story confirmed its accuracy (Holan 2008). Although it is difficult to determine how many people viewed the ad at the time, it generated quite a bit of buzz while costing the McCain campaign far less than would a comparable TV spot.

Campaigns are turning to social media platforms to overcome some of the limitations of traditional earned and paid media. Through social media, a candidate's supporters can be enlisted to reach out to their friends, raise money, and share information, bypassing news outlets. Digital ads may be microtargeted to individual voters whose political views and behavior have been revealed by their online activity. Rather than pay tens of thousands of dollars to run a 30-second spot on television, a campaign may post it—or longer, edgier videos—on You-Tube and encourage its supporters to share with their Facebook friends and Twitter followers. If the video is controversial or unusually clever, it might get covered in the news media or discussed on a talk show. As a result, the video can be viewed by thousands of voters without the campaign buying much if any airtime or arranging an interview with an antagonistic reporter.

Social media's importance stems in part from changes in the way people consume political information. The process is becoming *unbundled*. Rather than read a newspaper in the morning and watch the evening news—or even scan a media outlet's website—people are increasingly likely to consume individual stories from a variety of sources throughout the day. Sometimes they find individual items when they use Google or another search engine to search for a topic (e.g., "Barack Obama birth certificate,"), then click on the links. Increasingly, however, more and more voters are encountering individual news items and other political content on their Facebook newsfeed or Twitter feed. How that happens, and particularly the role campaigns play, is the subject of this chapter.

This chapter focuses on the four dominant social media outlets for campaign politics: Facebook, Twitter, YouTube, and email. All four qualify as social media because they *enable voters to create their own content and share it with others*. Each outlet functions in very different ways, and each emphasizes certain aspects of social media over others. In reality, the campaigns themselves actually provide much of the content that appears on social media—more so than users. They also foster much of the sharing. Even so, the communication modes exhibited on social media are very different than the clearly top-down processes that characterize the traditional earned and paid media strategies described in previous chapters. Indeed, social media outlets are strategically promising because they allow campaigns to:

- *Bypass traditional media outlets* and instead
- *Communicate directly with supporters*, who can be enlisted to
- *Do their own campaigning* by reaching out to friends, posting messages, sharing videos and other forms of content, and providing other forms of assistance to the candidates they support.

Much of social media's promise is rooted in its capacity for "peer-to-peer" communication. Under this notion, a candidate's supporters are most effective when they communicate with friends, acquaintances, colleagues—people with whom they share personal or professional ties. Thus, a college student who supports Rand Paul can communicate with fellow college students; a doctor to fellow doctors; a teacher to fellow teachers; a member of the family with other members of the family. Peer-to-peer campaigning can be powerful because the recipient is likely to relate to and trust the source. Because social media outlets so often entail communication among people with existing ties, they are conducive to peer-to-peer campaigning.

Facebook is the outlet that most comprehensively combines social media's potential assets, and its reach is impressive. Twitter provides a more top-down experience but seems to offer more political content as well as a mobile-friendly format. Social networks are less important for YouTube than the others, but YouTube may offer the most potential in terms of user-generated content. Email is less exciting technologically, yet serves as a powerful fundraising tool. As we will see, all four outlets offer a great deal of promise that campaigns are only beginning to realize.

Facebook

Facebook is a media behemoth. According to the Pew Research Center, 64 percent of US adults reported using Facebook in 2014. That compared with 16 percent for Twitter. Like Twitter, it has become an important medium for news. About three in ten adults report getting at least some of their news from Facebook. While other popular social media outlets—Pinterest (15 percent) and Instagram (12 percent), for example—also attract large overall audiences, these platforms are not significant news providers. And although Reddit is a news source for 62 percent of its users, its audience is tiny: only three percent of adults in 2013 (Matsa and Mitchell 2014).

Facebook users encounter political content in a number of ways. Most of it appears on the *newsfeed* located in the middle of the main Facebook page. The newsfeed is a constantly updated list of posts by "friends," "likes," and a few advertisers. A typical newsfeed contains plenty of non-political content: photos flaunting cute babies and goofy pets, eye-catching restaurant meals, celebratory family gatherings, and brag-worthy "don't you wish you were here?" trips to exotic places; links to news about celebrities and sports; complaints about the lousy weather, a bad day at the office, or a boring professor; amusing GIFs (brief, low-resolution video clips). At the top of the page, Facebook asks users to share "What's on your mind?" Many of the answers to that question have little to do with politics. But during election season—especially presidential years—newsfeeds will contain more posts that are relevant to—and are often driven by—candidates and their supporters.

Facebook's like function is key. When a user clicks on the like button associated with a particular Facebook page, posts from that page appear on the user's newsfeed. Users may receive news stories from a media outlet by clicking the like button associated with the source's Facebook page. If a user supports a candidate running for office, she may show her support by liking the candidate, which also ensures that the candidate's posts will appear on her newsfeed. Users also may like the Facebook pages of advocacy groups, political parties, and other political organizations. Many talk show hosts and other opinion-based media figures also have their own pages. The more political likes a user has, the more political content appears on their newsfeed.

Facebook friends also provide political content. Friends might post a status update touting a candidate they support or panning his or her opponent. These posts often feature links to a related news story or affirming commentary. A friend might share a video clip showing a candidate committing a gaffe. Or they might post material that casts a positive light on the candidate they support: a clip showing the candidate delivering an effective line in a speech, telling a funny joke at a campaign event, or shooting hoops. On Election Day, newsfeeds are filled with friends' "I voted" posts.

For campaigns, it is noteworthy that Facebook friends can range from lifelong soulmates to one-time acquaintances. They can be as close as family members (you can "friend" a parent) and as distant as a long-forgotten elementary school classmate. Facebook friends can be coworkers and classmates. As such, Facebook friend networks are unusually heterogeneous. This means that people are more likely to encounter a wider array of political viewpoints on Facebook than they do in their interpersonal, face-to-face networks, which tend to be more like-minded (Thorson, Vrega, and Kliger-Vilenchik 2015). Thus, Facebook is unique in that users are likely to encounter posts that present opinions unlike their own. This means that most Facebook users see posts about candidates from both major parties.

Facebook also serves as an outlet for reaching people who are otherwise disengaged. Many users encounter political content accidently, as a byproduct of simply being on Facebook. According to Pew, 78 percent of people who get news from Facebook do so inadvertently—i.e., when they are on Facebook for reasons other than seeking news (Mitchell et al. 2013). Users who consider themselves non-political probably have Facebook friends who are actively posting about the campaign. They can't help but encounter at least some campaign messaging.

Not all posts are treated equally. Facebook uses a formula for determining which posts are featured most prominently on users' newsfeeds. Frequently adjusted, the formula accounts for an array of predictors—for example, whether a mobile device is being used; the location of the device; users' other likes; and the number of likes the post has generated (Somaiya 2014a). This means that if a user likes a candidate, the newsfeed won't necessarily feature all of the candidate's posts in the order they were posted. Instead, it will highlight the posts that Facebook predicts the user is more likely to click on and spend time reading or watching. Among users' friends, the formula favors those whose previous status updates were liked or commented on by the user. Facebook ads are more likely to appear if the sponsor's page was liked by the user's friends. Facebook's goal on this front is to highlight posts that are more likely to yield *active engagement*. According to Facebook engineer Greg Marra, "we're saying, 'We think that of all the stuff you've connected yourself to, this is the stuff you'd be most interested in reading'" (Somaiya 2014a). "Click bait" headlines that trigger brief glances are less sought-after than they once were: the Facebook algorithm now accounts for how long users spend reading the post and how many users comment on or share it, not simply the number of likes or fleeting clicks (Somaiya 2014b).

For campaigns, Facebook's power stems not only from its vast reach, but its ability to communicate directly with supporters and enlist their help. Users who like the candidate's Facebook page are treated as supporters. At minimum, that means they will get updates from the campaign on their newsfeed. Campaigns use the newsfeed function in a variety of ways: to remind supporters to give money; to recruit them to make calls or knock on doors; to link to relevant news stories or editorials, including brief commentary by the candidate. Leading up to and on election day, supporters' newsfeeds are filled with reminders to vote. Campaigns also encourage their Facebook supporters to reach out to others. As with any Facebook page, users who already like the candidate are asked to invite their Facebook friends to like the page. In 2012, the Obama campaign took this a step further: they asked supporters for permission to scan their list of Facebook friends for persuadable voters. These friends saw content aimed at converting them into supporters. "Individuals fitting persuadable voter profiles were likely to see targeted content spilling into their newsfeeds from the campaign and their friends' Facebook posts" (Hendricks and Schill 2015: 3).

Campaign advertising appears in the form of "suggested" or "sponsored" posts. Aside from the labeling, sponsored posts appear on the newsfeed and are designed to look less like an ad and more like a standard status update from a liked page. Other Facebook ads appear in the right column on the main page. Campaigns use sponsored posts as an outlet for targeted messages based on user's Facebook data and behavior. This means that a user who likes Hillary Clinton is more likely to see targeted posts or ads supporting other Democratic candidates. Republican campaigns might target content toward users who like Fox News. College students might see more get-out-the-vote messaging than older users who need less encouragement to vote.

Facebook is notable for its capacity to give supporters tools for doing their own campaigning. For example, Facebook has a function for creating and publicizing events—fundraisers, for example—to people in their friend networks. Although Facebook networks can be pretty diverse, users tend to have many friends with whom they share something in common. When a user touts the virtues of a candidate on Facebook, people who know, relate to and trust them are likely to see it.

Facebook's capacity for interactivity and user-generated content provides many opportunities for innovation, but so far campaigns seem reluctant to give up control of messaging. In 2012, even the cutting-edge Obama campaign limited Facebook communication to "top-down promotion" of the candidate's message and voter mobilization rather than using it as a platform for meaningful interaction (Gerodimos and Justinussen 2014: 8). Posts tended to focus more on personality and character than the President's policy record. In the end, "only one out of 163 posts asked followers to consider what could be classified as a substantive question. Therefore, although the campaign successfully used Facebook to extend and mobilize its fan base, the strategic discourse did not encourage the creation of loops of feedback" (Gerodimos and Justinussen 2014: 17). This finding is consistent with a study by Jenny Bronstein (2013), who examined Facebook posts from the final three months of the 2012 presidential election. She found that posts tended to focus on a small number of non-controversial topics.

Campaigns have reasons to be cautious. Not everyone appreciates political posts. Many users are reluctant to share their views on Facebook, employing a "strategy of self-censorship, maintaining a polite silence, even on topics that they felt deeply about" (Thorson, Vrega, and Kliger-Vilenchik 2015: 81). According to one study, Facebook users are turned off by highly opinionated, pushy political rants (Thorson, Vrega, and Kliger-Vilenchik 2015). About 18 percent of social media users have "blocked, unfriended, or hidden someone on the site because the person either posted too much about politics, disagreed with political posts, or bothered friends with political posts." (Rainie and Smith 2012). Liberals may be more likely than conservatives to unfriend due to objectionable political content— perhaps because conservatives are more selective about their Facebook friendship networks to begin with (Mitchell et al. 2014). Overall, users express a preference for neutral political content. Yet the reality is that balanced posts are unlikely to get read (Thorson, Vrega, and Kliger-Vilenchik 2015).

What to do? Apparently users like posts that present political content in a witty or creative way, suggesting that clever humor on Facebook provides campaigns with "a way to get people to swallow the 'bitter pill' of politics" (Thorson, Vrega, and Kliger-Vilenchik 2015: 89). Perhaps as a result, many of the most memorable Facebook activity during election campaigns involves memes—often unflattering photos of candidates with funny captions. In 2012, when *Time* magazine published photos of Republican Vice Presidential candidate Paul Ryan lifting weights, many Facebook users saw a variety of captioned versions of the photos poking fun at Ryan's goofy facial expression and dated workout attire.

Facebook's potential power is demonstrated by the success of its "I voted" campaign. Since 2008, Election Day users have seen an "I voted" button at the top of their newsfeeds inviting them to click on the button once they cast a ballot. Once they did, an "I voted" announcement then appeared on their friends' newsfeeds. In a study of the 2010 election (Bond et al. 2012), researchers tested the effects of this campaign. As part of this study, the newsfeeds of nearly 61 million Facebook users contained five elements: a reminder that "Today is Election Day," a clickable "I Voted" button, a link to local polling places, a counter displaying number of FB users who had already reported voting, and profile photos of up to six Facebook friends who had reported voting. These users were compared with two groups of 600,000 users each. A control group received none of these messages. The other group saw everything except the photos of close friends who voted. The result? Self-reported turnout was slightly higher among users who got at least some of the vote messaging. But the photos of friends who voted seemed especially impactful. This suggested that although the informational messaging exerted some influence, what really mattered was the social pressure of close friends. The findings serve as a reminder that individual-level mobilization efforts can boost turnout (Gerber and Green 2000). It also reminds us that voting can be "contagious" between people with close ties (Nickerson 2008). And Facebook can foster that form of social pressure.

Twitter

Twitter is a very simple platform. It centers on "tweets"—brief, primarily text-based messages capped at 140 characters. Users may post their own tweets, read other people's tweets, or both. Similar to Facebook's news feed, the primary user interface is a list of posts. But rather than "friend" someone, users subscribe to other users' tweets by "following" them. A Twitter feed thus consists of a chronological list of tweets by people or groups being followed by the user—candidates and other politicians, journalists and other media figures, as well as celebrities, athletes, as well as friends and acquaintances.

Twitter's streamlined text-based format makes it a good fit for mobile devices and their small screens. But tweets are not limited to text. Twitter allows users to post photos and links to external web-based content such as videos, news stories, and websites. Users can also retweet messages that they would like to share with their followers—a process similar to "sharing" posts on Facebook.

Some tweets are labeled with hashtags. A hashtag is a word or phrase aimed at grouping together tweets that share a common topic. The label is preceded by the hash character on a keyboard commonly known as the pound sign (#)—for example, #RandPaul2016. Hashtags serve a variety of functions. They allow users to follow a topic that interests them by searching for identically tagged tweets. Sometimes users attempt to start a Twitter-based conversation on a topic by giving it a hashtag. Republicans did this during the 2014 midterm elections with #IAmARepublican, an effort to make GOP voters more relatable through first-hand testimonials on Twitter and other social media. Other hashtags seem aimed less at grouping tweets than at clever wordplay—#bindersfullofwomen, for example, which erupted on Twitter after Mitt Romney used the phrase "binders full of women" in response to a question about pay equity during the second presidential debate in 2012.

Whereas Facebook centers on horizontal communication among "friends," Twitter has become more of a vertical, top-down form of social media. Nearly half of Twitter users never tweet (Murphy 2014). For many users, Twitter is less of a social networking service and more of a highly targeted news aggregator—a phone-friendly platform for scrolling through news and other information that interests them based on the sources they follow. According to one study, Twitter users are driven by "information-seeking goals" as much as social media-type "social interaction motives" (Cozma 2015: 102). In politics, many of the most active, widely followed tweeters are journalists, media pundits, and talk show hosts. Plenty of rank-and-file citizens tweet. But many users' Twitter feeds are dominated by traditional content providers.

Compared with Facebook, Twitter's reach is small but highly engaged. Only 16 percent of adults in the U.S. reported using Twitter in 2013. But among those who do use Twitter, news is a top draw. About half of Twitter users get at least some news from Twitter (Matsa and Mitchell 2014a). And among users who report high levels of interest in politics, at least half of their tweets are political—twice the rate of highly engaged Facebook users (Gottfried 2014).

Campaigns have embraced Twitter in part because of the highly engaged nature of its user base. Many Twitter users are likely voters. Since so many of these users turn to Twitter for news, the platform allows campaigns to communicate with them directly, bypassing traditional news outlets. Naturally, users who "follow" a candidate's tweets are predisposed to support the candidate. Presumably many are devoted backers, and the odds of reaching uncommitted, persuadable voters are slim. But campaigns appreciate the ability to share information directly with likely supporters. During the 2012 debates, both the Obama and Romney campaigns used Twitter to reach out to followers by sharing links to relevant stories; elaborating on points raised by their candidate; fact-checking and responding in real time to attacks from the other side; creating hashtags to focus discussion on key favorable moments; and tweeting direct quotes from both candidates (Schill and Kirk 2015). Many users actively respond to this sort of activity. According to a study of Twitter and the 2012 GOP primaries, 40 percent of respondents said they retweeted or replied to candidate messages (Cozma 2015).

Twitter also serves as a versatile "earned media" tool. In Chapter 3, we examined the strategies and tools campaigns employ to "manage the news" through their relationships with media outlets. Twitter is conducive to many of these efforts. Its utility as an earned media tool stems from its popularity among political journalists. "Twitter is the central news source for the Washington-based political news establishment" (Hamby 2013: 4). That is because a typical journalist's Twitter feed provides a consolidated, constantly updated stream of posts from sources within the campaign, as well as competing news outlets. Breaking news, live reactions to events, scoops by competitors, timely announcements by the campaigns—it's all there on their phone, tablet or laptop—one need not leave the office or hotel room. The *New York Times'* Jonathan Martin described Twitter's importance to journalists covering the presidential campaigns in 2012:

> It's the gathering spot, it's the filing center, it's the hotel bar, it's the press conference itself all in one … It's the central gathering place now for the political class during campaigns but even after campaigns. It's even more than

that. It's become the real-time political wire. That's where you see a lot of breaking news. That's where a lot of judgments are made about political events, good, bad or otherwise.

(Hamby 2013: 24)

Campaigns realize Twitter's importance to journalists and respond accordingly. In 2012, both Obama and Romney campaigns

viewed Twitter as a means of influencing journalists in a world where content quickly moves across platforms, news unfolds in rapidly revised versions, what happens on Twitter informs what takes shape in other mediums, and winning the news cycle is now defined all the way down to the half hour.

(Kreiss 2014)

Campaigns exploit the fact that Twitter serves as a "second screen" for journalists during live campaign events such as debates, speeches, and conventions (the first screen is a television). During a debate, for example, journalists are doing what many media-savvy citizens are doing: watching the event live on TV while monitoring reactions on Twitter using their laptop, tablet or phone. Knowing this, campaigns strategically "live-tweet" the event partly in an effort to influence media coverage—both during and after the event. When their candidate lands a hit, they tweet about it. When their opponent stumbles or commits a gaffe, they tweet about it. When a journalist or pundit tweets a positive comment, they retweet it. They fact-check their opponents' arguments with links to supporting evidence. Hashtags are employed to draw attention to noteworthy moments.

Campaigns live-tweet debates partly because they perceive that journalists are using Twitter as a "giant focus group of other journalists where the constant stream of comments can coalesce into major themes or issues" (Schill and Kirk 2015: 207). Campaigns also monitor journalists' tweets to anticipate emerging storylines even before the debate is over. Who do journalists think won the debate? What were the key newsworthy moments? Did anyone commit a newsworthy gaffe? Traditionally these questions are usually explored in the "spin room," where reporters and campaign spokespersons gather for post-debate interviews (see Chapter 3). But in 2012, "the spin room was on Twitter, where journalists, campaign communications staff, and influential citizen elites debated a co-created narrative about what happened" (Schill and Kirk 2015: 206). Romney adviser Eric Fehrnstrom said Twitter "made it easier to spin" the debates partly because the campaigns could respond to media storylines, positive or negative, before they solidified (Hamby 2013: 27).

Not surprisingly, then, Twitter is a key tool in campaigns' "rapid response" arsenal. It enables them to respond instantly to opponents' attacks as well as potentially damaging news stories. For example, as a Republican Presidential candidate in 2012, Jon Huntsman set up a "Reality Room" on Twitter (@Rea-lityRoom) to serve as a "campaign reality check" on tweets, blog posts, and media content perceived as harmful to the campaign. Unfortunately for campaign operatives, Twitter's speed also feeds the expectation among reporters that responses should be instant, not merely rapid. An adviser to South Carolina Governor Nikki Haley complained that rapid response is now

> defined by a reporter who calls and says, "I'm going to post in five minutes, and I need a response" … Often, the calls come when he's away from his computer, or driving to the grocery store, or in a meeting, or just too busy to come up with a publishable response in that exact moment that doesn't include a filthy word.
>
> *(Hamby 2013: 37)*

Indeed, the speed can be breathtaking. On Twitter, the storyline about Obama's lackluster performance during the first 2012 debate solidified even before the event was over. *BuzzFeed*'s Ben Smith declared Romney the winner less than 45 minutes into the 90-minute debate (Schill and Kirk 2015). When a candidate makes a gaffe, it spreads instantaneously, even before the campaigns can respond. The quality of information suffers as a result. Reporters sometimes break news on Twitter even before the full story gets written and fact-checked. For the sake of speed, a story might be based on a single one-sided anonymous source. Stories based on inaccurate information sometimes get retweeted by established journalists, unjustifiably enhancing the story's credibility. Mistakes eventually get corrected, but only after the misinformation has been widely tweeted and retweeted.

Twitter enables campaigns to bypass the media hierarchy. They no longer need the *New York Times* to get exposure. "A link is a link, dude" said Romney campaign manager Matt Rhoades (Hamby 2013: 31). According to CNN reporter Peter Hamby, in 2012 "an online story, no matter how biased or thinly reported, had a URL that could be peddled to other news outlets, linked to the *Drudge Report* and, most importantly, pumped directly into the Twitter feeding frenzy where influencers lived" (Hamby 2013: 31). On Twitter, a storyline's importance isn't determined by editors, producers and other traditional media gatekeepers. Instead, it's measured by the number of tweets, retweets, and hashtags.

Campaigns sometimes chafe at the level of detail on Twitter. Much of what reporters tweet about is trivial stuff. Every aspect of the campaign is fair game for a tweet. Reporters covering the 2012 Romney campaign tweeted about the quality of food served on the press bus, their lack of access to the candidate, and the campaign plane breaking down. The Romney campaign was not happy. Surely advisers to Romney's GOP rival Michelle Bachmann weren't happy either when reporters tweeted about what medication the candidate takes for her migraines (Enda 2011). In some ways, there is nothing new about this. As we saw in Chapter 1, the media have long been criticized for focusing more on small-bore "process" or "horse race" type stories than substantive policy debates. Reporter Theodore White, who wrote a pioneering series of books micro-detailing the presidential campaigns of the 1960s, once expressed regret for inventing "a style of political analysis that went to great lengths to describe the brand of cereal that candidates ate for breakfast" (Miller 1999: 403). Today, although reporters may not be tweeting about the candidate's favorite brand, it would not be surprising to see them tweet complaints about the quality of the cereal being served on the campaign plane.

BOX 5.1 (TWITTER) BIRDS ON THE BUS

Timothy Crouse's classic non-fiction book *Boys on the Bus* chronicled the experiences of reporters covering the 1972 presidential campaign between Richard Nixon and George McGovern. Nearly all of the reporters were male and they traveled by bus—hence the name. Four decades later, what has changed?

Twitter, for one. On the one hand, news outlets still assign reporters to follow major candidates around as they travel the country—although many save money by assigning inexperienced, underpaid "jack of all trades" youngsters who both report and shoot video. The campaigns themselves still handle many of the travel logistics—part of the "care and feeding" strategies described in Chapter 3.

On the other hand, Twitter enables a media outlet to cover a campaign without paying to send an experienced reporter to follow the candidate full time. How so? At least two reasons. One, the campaigns tweet minute-by-minute updates about what their candidate is saying and doing, minimizing the need for a reporter to be present. Two, many of the reporters and journalists who *are* on the bus also tweet about what they see and hear. Thus, a media outlet can produce a detail-filled story without actually being there. All of the reporting has been shared on Twitter.

For news outlets, Twitter-based coverage saves money without sacrificing much in terms of the quality of coverage. After all, the "boys on the bus" produced *pack journalism*—a phrase coined by the book's author to describe the groupthink that occurs when journalists work together too closely, sharing observations and ideas. Even today, the "traveling press" often produce stories that focus excessively on trivial details rather than the broader context. They do so in part because the campaigns provide so little direct access to the candidates, limiting reporters to scripted events and photo ops. The costs alone are staggering. In 2012, it could cost as much as $10,000 a week to assign a reporter to follow either the campaign of Mitt Romney or his vice presidential pick, Paul Ryan (Hamby 2013). Campaigns seem unhappy with the status quo as well. They resent having to make travel arrangements for reporters who reward them with negative stories. Sometimes it hardly seems worthwhile to either the campaign or the media.

Yet Twitter-based coverage can only do so much. 140-character tweets cannot possibly replace first-hand accounts supplied by an experienced, full-time reporter. While it is true that the traveling press focus on trivialities, they also produce plenty of colorful reports that provide in-depth insight into the candidates and their operations—not easy to do when relying on a Twitter feed. In addition, since the Twitter conversation is so often dominated by journalists and political insiders, it may contribute to pack journalism just as much as "boys on the bus" arrangements do. Apparently reporters covering the campaigns spend a lot of time following up on what other reporters are tweeting about, while their editors prod them with "Do we have this?" emails and messages.

Neither journalists nor campaigns seem nostalgic for the good old days on the bus. Twitter has become an essential tool for journalists covering election campaigns. But its limitations remind us what is lost when media outlets lack the resources they need to invest in good reporting.

Sources: Crouse 1973; Enda 2011; Hamby 2013

YouTube

YouTube is one of the most popular websites in the world. More than half of Americans use the site (Anderson and Caumont 2014). There are other video-sharing platforms but YouTube dominates the market. Its appeal lies in the ability for anybody to post a video on just about anything for free. Launched in 2005, its emergence coincided with the advent of low-cost, user-friendly video filming on smart phones and other devices. In a matter of minutes, a user can film a video on their phone and upload it onto their YouTube page. YouTube has thus fostered both the production and consumption of online video (Ridout, Fowler and Branstetter 2012).

For campaigns, YouTube is a platform for posting all kinds of video content without paying for airtime on television. It has become standard practice for campaigns to post their 30- and 60-second TV ads on their YouTube page, where voters can watch (and share them) for free. It is also possible to post lengthier videos ranging from extended versions of standard TV spots to documentary-type programs about the candidate or her/his opponents. When Newt Gingrich challenged Mitt Romney for the Republican presidential nomination in 2012, a Super PAC supporting him produced "King of Bain," a 27-minute documentary-style video that attacked Romney for eliminating jobs while he ran the private equity firm Bain Capital. In 2010, Carly Fiorina's Senate campaign posted the infamous "Demon Sheep" ad, a bizarre three-minute video attacking Republican primary opponent Tom Campbell for being a "Fiscal Conservative in Name Only." At the ad's 2:26 mark, the "demon sheep" appears: a man in a sheep's costume with glowing red eyes, hiding among innocent sheep grazing in a meadow—"a wolf in sheep's clothing," the narrator says, "Has He Fooled You?" the on-screen text asks. In terms of both length and weirdness, this is not the sort of ad commonly seen on television.

The 2008 election was called the YouTube election by pundits, journalists, commentators, citizens (Towner and Dulio 2012). That is in part because the Obama campaign did so much with it. Whereas most of McCain's videos were 30-second spots that could have run on television, the Obama campaign also posted candidate speeches, celebrity endorsements, and brief documentary-type programs (Cortese and Proffitt 2012). It posted training videos for volunteers onto YouTube for anyone to watch. One example was a three-minute "How to Canvass in Nevada" video, during which a field organizer offers advice on attire, demeanor, safety, procedures, how to use the "script" and "walk list," what to say to voters, and—for out-of-staters—how to pronounce Nevada correctly ("I hAd a blAst in NevAda"). The Obama campaign also posted lengthy programs focused on supporters telling their "stories." One 20-minute video focused on Joshua Stroman, a South Carolina college student and campaign volunteer who turned his life around after landing in jail. One scene shows Joshua chatting with Obama, who then singles him out in a campaign speech as an example of a "story of going through hard times, but overcoming them." The most viewed campaign video in 2008 was "Yes We Can," a four-and-a-half minute music video by Black Eyed Peas frontman will.i.am that featured numerous celebrities singing the words of an Obama speech. Most U.S. Senate candidates also used YouTube in 2008, albeit primarily to host 30-second spots and clips from traditional campaign events and debates (Klotz 2010). By 2012, a YouTube page was standard for campaigns of all levels. That year, YouTube launched Elections Hub, a site that live-streamed nationally televised debates, both parties' conventions, as well as video reports by news organizations ranging from *The New York Times* to *BuzzFeed*.

YouTube's motto is "Broadcast Yourself," which underlines its original emphasis on amateur clips posted by ordinary citizens rather than by campaign organizations and traditional media outlets. Scholars call this "user-generated content." Early election-related approaches include video blogs, or "vlogs"— monologues delivered by a person facing a camera, in this context either raving or ranting about one or more candidates. In 2008, Obama supporters posted videos parodying two attack ads aired by his opponents: Hillary Clinton's "3 AM" spot, which raised questions about Obama's national security experience, and John McCain's "Celebrity" ad, which mocked Obama's fame. The spoofs were "mashups" combining clips from the originals ads, stock images, and comedic footage produced by the user (Tryon 2008). During the 2012 campaign for the Republican nomination, users posted videos of themselves acting as citizen journalists who interview candidates and film campaign events (Klotz 2012).

As with all social media, sharing is crucial. Videos may be posted for free, but their impact is limited if potential supporters are not watching them. This is where other social media outlets come in. YouTube and other video-hosting platforms now make it relatively easy for users to post a link to the video in a Facebook update, a Tweet, an email, or other social media mechanism. Campaign-sanctioned videos rarely "go viral"—"Yes We Can" was an exception—but "views" and "likes" can increase by the thousands when supporters share them with their friends and followers. Campaigns play a crucial role in fostering video sharing through other social media platforms as well as the news media (Ridout, Fowler and Branstetter 2012).

Videos of candidates committing gaffes frequently do go viral. Campaigns now hire "trackers" to film opponents speaking at campaign events in case the opposing candidate says or does something embarrassing, offensive or silly. The use of trackers accelerated in the wake of a few high-profile gaffes that made their way onto YouTube. The most famous case was Republican Senator George Allen's "Macaca" gaffe in 2006. Running for reelection, Allen was being tracked by S.R. Siddarth, who worked for Democratic opponent Jim Webb. At a campaign rally on August 11, Allen recognized Siddarth among a crowd of supporters, pointed to him called him "Macaca," saying "Hey, let's give a welcome to Macaca here, welcome to America and the real world of Virginia." It is unclear what Allen meant by this: Macaca is a racial epithet, but an obscure one, and Allen's larger aim seemed to be to underscore his opponent's decision to attend a fundraiser with "Hollywood movie moguls" rather than interact with "real Virginians" (Karpf 2010: 159). But the gaffe reinforced Allen's reputation for racial insensitivity, and *The Washington Post* ran a front-page story about it. Three days after the event occurred, the video appeared on YouTube. Eventually, 75 versions of the clip were posted by a variety of different users (Fernandez 2006). Widely shared by email, on social media and the blogosphere, the video received hundreds of thousands of hits and contributed to the demise of Allen's presidential aspirations (he also lost the election).

A different 2006 Senate race similarly raised YouTube's profile in campaign circles. Montana Senator Conrad Burns was running for reelection, and a campaign worker for his opponent John Tester posted a series of damning videos onto YouTube. One depicted Burns nodding off during a meeting in his home state. In another, Burns can be heard referring to "this little fella who does our main-tenance work around the house, he's from Guatemala." A third video showed Burns praising U.S. troops fighting an enemy who is a "taxi cab driver in the daytime but a killer at night." The videos underlined Burns' image as being old, cranky and clueless. While it is impossible to attribute Burns' loss to the videos, they—along with Allen's "Macaca" clips—signaled the emergence of a new mechanism for negative campaigning on social media.

YouTube's capacity for creative, user-generated content raised hopes about a more open and diverse campaign communication environment, but early research has been discouraging. A study of 2008 Senate races indicated that YouTube mostly served as "a repository for ads produced by the candidates and parties" as well as repurposed video from traditional modes of communication: speeches, campaign events, and debate clips. In other words, the YouTube presence of Senate candidates was "dominated by candidates themselves communicating in traditional formats supplemented by the familiar products of the mainstream media" (Klotz 2010: 122). Rather than democratizing electioneering, YouTube merely provided another platform for top-down communication. Even the widely viewed "Obama Girl" video was professionally produced. Ostensibly, the video was a first-person tribute by a young woman singing about her crush on then-Senator Obama. But the truth is the video was the brainchild of an advertising executive, performed by a professional singer, and lip-synched by a professional actress and model.

Recent developments suggest more variety and experimentation. In a study of campaigns for the U.S. Senate in 2010, online ads sponsored by private citizens garnered significantly more views on average than online spots by interest groups, offering "some reason to doubt the claim that user-generated content is simply ignored" (Ridout, Fowler, and Branstetter 2012: 15). By 2012, YouTube was "realizing some of its potential for creating a diverse campaign environment" (Klotz 2012: 17). According to one study, the most viewed YouTube video during the 2012 primaries was a citizen-filmed clip showing an eight-year-old whispering to Michelle Bachmann that "my mom is gay but she doesn't need any fixing." Only two of the 80 most-viewed videos during the 2012 Republican primaries were standard 30-second ads (Klotz 2012).

Email

"I will be outspent" raised $2.5 million. "Some scary numbers" raised $1.9 million. These were subject lines for the top two fundraising email messages from the Obama campaign during the 2012 election. The text of these emails pleaded with the recipient to contribute to the campaign … or else. Leading off the "I will be outspent" email was a message from the President that "I will be the first president in modern history to be outspent in his reelection campaign, if things continue as they have so far." Anyone who shared their email address with the campaign was inundated with messages like this throughout the campaign. Supporters complained, and Jon Stewart mocked the emails on his show, but they were effective: according to the Obama campaign, most of the $690 million raised on line came from fundraising emails (Green 2012).

Email is less flashy than other social media outlets, but it has the widest potential reach. Nine out of 10 online adults in the U.S. use email on a regular basis (Purcell 2011). Campaigns are thus eager to collect email addresses of existing supporters and persuadable voters alike. Theoretically, this could enable direct communication throughout the campaign and beyond. Anyone on the campaign's email list could receive not only fundraising pitches, but also requests to volunteer for canvassing efforts; links to videos on YouTube, the campaign's website, and favorable news stories or commentary; and reminders to vote and encourage their friends to do the same.

Email's capacity for social sharing is impressive. This is where email forwarding comes in. As with other forms of social media (especially Facebook), supporters on the email list are enlisted to help the campaign reach out to people in their online networks—in this case, their email contacts. Campaign-generated emails often have links labeled something like "send/forward to a friend." Some recipients do exactly that, and the effects of email forwarding on second-hand recipients can be dramatic (Cornfield 2004), presumably because the forwarder is trusted as a source of political information.

Despite its potential, however, email still serves primarily as a top-down fundraising tool for campaigns. In 2012, emails from the Romney and Obama campaigns did little more than promote their own respective candidates with information about the horserace and links to fundraising applications (Williams and Maiorescu 2015). Given email's fundraising successes, perhaps campaigns are reluctant to dilute its effectiveness with messaging about anything else.

Conclusion

Email and other forms of social media outlets can be impactful campaign communication tools. After all, they provide a platform for interpersonal communication among connected people, many of whom know and trust each other. Decades of research have shown that this form of communication can be very powerful—much more so than relatively impersonal mass media (Lazarsfeld, Berelson and Gaudet 1968). Social media outlets carry messages aimed at not only reinforcing existing predispositions and mobilizing supporters, but also indirect persuasion of people who have not yet made up their minds. Recall from Chapter 4 that under John Zaller's RAS theory, attitude change happens only when individuals both *receive* and *accept* messages. With social media, persuasion is possible because the messages come from credible and trusted opinion leaders—Facebook friends, for example—increasing the likelihood of not only reception but also acceptance of the message. Vaccari's interviews with political consultants indicate that campaigns realize this potential (Vaccari 2012).

Yet campaigns are only beginning to scratch the surface. Facebook, Twitter, YouTube and email each have their own particular limitations, which were described earlier. Other concerns can be applied to social media in general. Campaigns may tout social media's potential for spreading the word about their candidate, but the reality is that much of the messaging centers on attacking their opponents. In 2012, for example, negative tweets about both Obama and Romney far outnumbered positive tweets (Mitchell and Hitlin 2013). During the Republican primaries, negative campaign ads were far more likely to be viewed on YouTube than positive ads (Groshek and Brookes 2015).

Social media provide plenty of opportunities to encounter political content. But will potential voters actively read or watch? Not always. There is some evidence that users who passively encounter content through social media are less engaged with the information than people who actively seek it out. According to a Pew study

> direct visitors—those who type in the news outlet's specific address (URL) or have the address bookmarked—spend much more time on that news site, view many more pages of content and come back far more often than visitors who arrive from a search engine or a Facebook referral.
>
> (Mitchell, Jurkowitz, and Olmstead 2014)

Specifically, among users visiting a news site from a laptop or desktop computer, direct visitors spent an average of 4:36 minutes on each site. That compared with about 1:41 minutes if clicked on the site via Facebook and 1:42 minutes if via a search engine.

This may explain why, according to one study, people who used social media for news during the early 2012 GOP primaries and caucuses were no more knowledgeable about politics than anyone else, and people who use social media as a primary source of news were even less knowledgeable (Baumgartner, Morris and Morris 2015). These findings are consistent with a study that coupled survey research with content analysis of political groups on Facebook, which found "that political Facebook group users, in general, often do not share much new information and the information they do share tends to be somewhat inaccurate, incoherent, or not very well supported with evidence" (Conroy, Feezell and Guerero 2012: 1543). Other studies report similarly discouraging results (e.g., Towner and Dulio 2015).

Campaigns also have yet to fully realize social media's potential for cultivating more active, innovative relationships with volunteers, supporters and voters. A study of social media use by the Obama and Romney campaigns found some evidence of "collaboration"—i.e., asking supporters and volunteers to help out, but little evidence of "openness"—disclosing information and sharing positive/negative thoughts—or "co-creation"—inviting supporters to shape campaign and systematically inviting feedback. "In the end, digital and social media might largely constitute another set of channels and platforms for communication rather than a revolution in terms of overall campaign strategies" (Svensson, Kiousis and Strömbäck 2015: 42). Indeed, for many campaigns, it could be that social media tools remain mere "extensions of traditional campaigns activities like fundraising, organizing volunteers, and identifying and turning out voters" (Towner and Dulio 2015: 73).

Perhaps that is enough. At relatively low cost, social media allow campaigns to communicate with supporters and enlist their support in sharing content, reaching new voters, and raising money. Although there is plenty of room for innovation, campaigns may be content with social media's capacity to help them do what they already do, only slightly better.

References

Anderson, Monica, and Andrea Caumont. 2014. "How social media is reshaping the news." Pew Research Center, Sept 24. http://www.pewresearch.org/fact-tank/2014/09/24/how-social-media-is-reshaping-news/.

Baumgartner, Jody C., David S. Morris, and Jonathan S. Morris. 2015. "Of Networks and Knowledge: Young Adults and the Early 2012 Republican Presidential Primaries and Caucuses." In *Presidential Campaigning and Social Media: An Analysis of the 2012 Campaign*, ed. John Allen Hendricks and Dan Schill. New York: Oxford University Press.

Bond, Robert M., Christopher J. Fariss, Jason J. Jones, Adam D.I. Kramer, Cameron Marlow, Jamie E. Settle, and James H. Fowler. 2012. "A 61-million-person Experiment in Social Influence and Political Mobilization," *Nature* 489 (13 September): 295–298.

Bronstein, Jenny. 2013. "Like me! Analyzing the 2012 Presidential Candidates' Facebook Pages." *Online Information Review* 37(2): 173–192.

Conroy, Meredth, Jessica T. Feezell, and Mario Guerrero. 2012. "Facebook and Political Engagment: A Study of Online Political Group Membership and Offline Political Engagement." *Computers in Human Behavior* 28: 1535–1546.

Cornfield, Michael. 2004. *Politics Moves Online: Campaigning and the Internet*. Century Foundation Press.

Cortese, Juliann, and Jennifer Proffitt. 2012. "Looking Back as We Prepare to Move Forward: US Presidential Candidates' Adoption of YouTube." *Cyberpsychology, Behavior, and Social Networking* 15(12): 693–697.

Cozma, Raluca. 2015. "Uses and Gratifications of Following Candidates' Twitter Campaigns during the 2012 U.S. Primaries." In *Presidential Campaigning and Social Media: An Analysis of the 2012 Campaign*, ed. John Allen Hendricks and Dan Schill. New York: Oxford University Press.

Crouse, Timothy. 1973. *The Boys on the Bus*. New York: Random House.

Enda, Jodi. 2011. "Campaign Coverage in a Time of Twitter." *American Journalism Review* (Oct./Nov.). http://ajrarchive.org/Article.asp?id=5134.

Fernandez, Raul. 2006 "Uploading American Politics." *Washington Post*, Dec. 9. http://www.washingtonpost.com/wp-dyn/content/article/2006/12/08/AR2006120801306.html.

Gerber, Alan S., and Donald P. Green. 2000. "The Effects of Canvassing, Telephone Calls, and Direct Mail on Voter Turnout: A Field Experiment." *The American Political Science Review* 94(3): 653–663.

Gerodimos, Romay, and Jákup Justinussen. 2014. "Obama's 2012 Facebook Campaign: Political Communication in the Age of the Like Button." *Journal of Information Technology & Politics* 00: 1–20. DOI: 10.1080/19331681.2014.982266.

Gottfried, Jeffrey. 2014. "Facebook and Twitter as Political Forums: Two Different Dynamics." Pew Research Center, Nov. 12. http://www.pewresearch.org/fact-tank/2014/11/12/facebook-and-twitter-as-political-forums-two-different-dynamics/.

Green, Joshua. 2012. "The Science Behind Those Obama Campaign E-Mails." *Bloomberg Business*, Nov. 29. http://www.bloomberg.com/bw/articles/2012-11-29/the-science-behind-those-obama-campaign-e-mails.

Groshek, Jacob, and Stephanie Brookes. 2015. "YouTube/OurTube/TheirTube: Official and Online Campaigns Advertising, Negativity, and Popularity." In *Presidential Campaigning and Social Media: An Analysis of the 2012 Campaign*, ed. John Allen Hendricks and Dan Schill. New York: Oxford University Press.

Hamby, Peter. 2013. "Did Twitter Kill the Boys on the Bus? Searching for a Better Way to Cover a Campaign." Discussion Paper #D-80, Joan Shorenstein Center on the Press, Politics and Public Policy, Boston, MA.

Hendricks, John Allen, and Dan Schill. 2015. "The Presidential Campaign of 2012: New Media Technologies Used to Interact with the Electorate." In *Presidential Campaigning and Social Media: An Analysis of the 2012 Campaign*, ed. John Allen Hendricks and Dan Schill. New York: Oxford University Press.

Holan, Angie Drobnic. 2008. "Another Flap over Flip-flops." *Tampa Bay Times*, Jan. 28. http://www.politifact.com/truth-o-meter/article/2008/jan/28/another-flap-over-flip-flops/.

Karpf, David. 2010. "Macaca Moments Reconsidered: Electoral Panopticon or Netroots Mobilization?" *Journal of Information Technology & Politics* 7(2–3): 143–162.

Klotz, Robert J. 2012. "The Intermittent YouTube Electoral Presence of Citizens and Candidates." Paper presented at the annual meeting of the Midwest Political Association, Chicago, IL.

Klotz, Robert J. 2010. "The Sidetracked 2008 YouTube Senate Campaign." *Journal of Information Technology & Politics* 7(2–3): 110–123.

Kreiss, Daniel. 2014. "Monkey Cage: The Real Story about how the Obama and Romney Campaigns used Twitter." *Washington Post*, Dec. 9. http://www.washingtonpost.com/blogs/monkey-cage/wp/2014/12/09/the-real-story-about-how-the-obama-and-romney-campaigns-used-twitter/.

Lazarsfeld, Paul, Bernard Berelson, and Hazel Gaudet. 1968. *The People's Choice: How the Voter Makes Up His Mind in a Presidential Campaign*, 3rd edition. New York: Columbia University Press.

Matsa, Katerina E. and Amy Mitchell. 2014. "8 Key Takeaways about Social Media and News." Pew Research Center, March 26. http://www.journalism.org/2014/03/26/8-key-takeaways-about-social-media-and-news/.

Miller, John E. 1999. "The Making of Theodore H. White: The Making of the President 1960." *Presidential Studies Quarterly* 29(2): 389–405.

Mitchell, Amy, and Paul Hitlin. 2013. "Twitter Reaction to Events Often at Odds with Overall Public Opinion." Pew Research Center, March 4. http://www.pewresearch.org/2013/03/04/twitter-reaction-to-events-often-at-odds-with-overall-public-opinion/.

Mitchell, Amy, Jeffrey Gottfried, Jocelyn Kiley, and Katerina Eva Matsa. 2014. "Political Polarization and Media Habits." Pew Research Center, Oct. 21. http://www.journalism.org/2014/10/21/political-polarization-media-habits/.

Mitchell, Amy, Mark Jurkowitz, and Kenneth Olmstead. 2014. "Social, Search and Direct: Pathways to Digital News." Pew Research Center, March 13. http://www.journalism.org/2014/03/13/social-search-direct/.

Mitchell, Amy, Jocelyn Kiley, Jeffrey Gottfried, and Emily Guskin. 2013. "The Role of News on Facebook." Pew Research Center, Oct. 24. http://www.journalism.org/2013/10/24/the-role-of-news-on-facebook/.

Murphy, David. 2014. "44 Percent of Twitter Accounts Have Never Tweeted." *PC Magazine*, April 13. http://www.pcmag.com/article2/0,2817,2456489,00.asp.

Nickerson, D.W. 2008. "Is Voting Contagious? Evidence from Two Field Experiments." *American Political Science Review* 102: 49–57.

Purcell, Kristen. 2011. "Search and Email Still Top the List of Popular Online Activities." Pew Research Center, Aug. 9. http://www.pewinternet.org/2011/08/09/search-and-email-still-top-the-list-of-most-popular-online-activities/.

Rainie, Lee, and Aaron Smith. 2012. "Politics on Social Networking Sites." Pew Research Center's Internet and American Life Project. Sept 4. http://pewinternet.org/Reports/2012/Politics-on-SNS.aspx.

Ridout, Travis N., Erika Franklin Fowler, and John Branstetter. 2012 "Political Advertising in the 21st Century: The Influence of the YouTube Ad." Paper prepared for the annual meeting of the Western Political Science Association, March 22–24, Portland, Oregon.

Schill, Dan, and Rita Kirk. 2015. "Issue Debates in 140 Characters: Online Talk Surrounding the 2012 Debates." In *Presidential Campaigning and Social Media: An Analysis of the 2012 Campaign*, ed. John Allen Hendricks and Dan Schill. New York: Oxford University Press.

Somaiya, Ravi. 2014a. "How Facebook is Changing the Ways Its Users Consume Journalism." *The New York Times*, Oct. 26. http://www.nytimes.com/2014/10/27/business/media/how-facebook-is-changing-the-way-its-users-consume-journalism.html?_r=0.

Somaiya, Ravi. 2014b. "Facebook Takes Steps Against 'Click Bait' Articles." *The New York Times*, Aug. 25. http://www.nytimes.com/2014/08/26/business/media/facebook-takes-steps-against-click-bait-articles.html.

Svensson, Emma, Spiro Kiousis, and Jesper Strömbäck. 2015. "Creating a Win-Win Situation? Relationship Cultivation and the Use of Social Media in the 2012 Election." In *Presidential Campaigning and Social Media: An Analysis of the 2012 Campaign*, ed. John Allen Hendricks and Dan Schill. New York: Oxford University Press.

Thorson, Kjerstin, Emily K. Vrega, and Neta Kliger-Vilenchik. 2015. "Don't Push Your Opinions on Me: Young Citizens and Political Etiquette on Facebook." In *Presidential Campaigning and Social Media: An Analysis of the 2012 Campaign*, ed. John Allen Hendricks and Dan Schill. New York: Oxford University Press.

Towner, Terri L., and David A. Dulio. 2015. "Technology Takeover? Campaign Learning during the 2012 Presidential Election." In *Presidential Campaigning and Social Media: An Analysis of the 2012 Campaign*, ed. John Allen Hendricks and Dan Schill. New York: Oxford University Press.

Towner, Terri L., and David A. Dulio. 2012 "New Media and Political Marketing in the United States: 2012 and Beyond." *Journal of Political Marketing* 11(1–2): 95–119.

Towner, Terri L., and David A. Dulio. 2011. "An Experiment of Campaign Effects during the YouTube Election." *New Media & Society* 13(4): 626–644.

Tryon, Chuck. 2008. "Pop Politics: Online Parody Videos, Intertextuality, and Political Participation." *Popular Communication: The International Journal of Media and Culture* 6(4): 209–213.

Vaccari, Cristian. 2012. "From Echo Chamber to Persuasive Device? Rethinking the Role of the Internet in Campaigns." *New Media & Society* 15(1): 109–127.

Williams, Andrew P., and Roxana Maiorescu. 2015. "Evaluating Textual and Technical Interactivity in Candidate Email Messages during the 2012 U.S. Presidential Campaign." In *Presidential Campaigning and Social Media: An Analysis of the 2012 Campaign*, ed. John Allen Hendricks and Dan Schill. New York: Oxford University Press.

CONCLUSION

The 2016 election was going to be different for Hillary Clinton. When she lost the Democratic nomination to Barack Obama in 2008, her campaign was criticized for many shortcomings: poor media relations, staff infighting, wasteful spending, and stale communication practices just to name a few. Eight years later, her campaign was determined to show the real Hillary: the down-to-earth grand-mother beloved by her friends for her sense of normalcy, kindness and generosity (Leibovich 2015). It would focus its earn media strategies on local outlets, but also repair Clinton's famously acrimonious relationship with the national media. It would surpass even the groundbreaking Obama campaigns in terms of social media outreach and innovation. Rather than blow most of its money on television spots, it would invest in microtargeted digital ads and data-driven fieldwork.

The campaign achieved many of these goals. Its field effort was particularly innovative. But in terms of Clinton's relationship with the national media, the 2016 effort proved to be more of the same. As usual, she kept journalists at arm's length. Like all candidates, she relied heavily on tightly managed photo ops as well as house parties and other events that kept reporters at a distance. Reporters complained that she rarely took their questions during these events. Their frustration was crystalized at a July 4th parade in New Hampshire, during which campaign officials corralled reporters and cameras behind a white rope. Photos of the scene "became the day's takeaway, at least in the national media: proof, supposedly, of Clinton's running scared from the 'tough questions,' thwarting press freedom on this day of our independence" (Leibovich 2015: 55).

Perhaps Clinton's caution was justifiable. During the 2014–2015 pre-primary stage of the race, the tone of her news coverage ranged from tepid to harsh. As the familiar frontrunner for the Democratic nomination, she lacked the novelty necessary for a compelling story. By journalism standards, she was old news. Her policy speeches got some press, but much of her news coverage focused on lagging polls numbers, the "enthusiasm gap" between her supporters and those of Democratic opponent Bernie Sanders, and—ironically—her struggles with the national media. Early in the race, she was subjected to classic feeding frenzy-type media coverage of the revelation that she used a private email account for government business during her tenure as Secretary of State. In short, Clinton's 2016 earned media strategy appeared to be no more satisfying than it was in 2008.

Clinton's media problems were exacerbated by major changes in the broader communication environment. Super PACs allied with the Republican Party were confident that she would win the Democratic nomination, freeing them to run ads and post tweets against her more than a year before the general election. For example, a two-minute online ad posted in April 2015 by the America Rising PAC touched on the email controversy, the 2012 attack on the U.S. consulate in Benghazi, and Clinton's claim that she and her husband had left the White House "dead broke." Conservative groups also tweeted critiques of Clinton's connections to Wall Street and New York Mayor Bill de Blasio (Parker and Corasanati 2015). Conservative media also hammered Clinton. Fox News and other conservative media outlets sustained coverage of the Benghazi controversy long after traditional news outlets lost interest in the story. Eventually the Benghazi story beget the email controversy: it was the Republican-controlled House committee investigating the attack that discovered the existence of Clinton's personal email account. *The New York Times*, long accused of exaggerating Clinton malfeasances, botched a story reporting that Clinton was under criminal investigation for the emails—a claim that turned out to be false (Ornstein 2015). Even relatively friendly media outlets such as the *Huffington Post* seemed more excited about Bernie Sanders, who challenged Clinton for the Democratic nomination from the party's left flank.

Like all candidates for elected office, Clinton was operating in a media environment that had been transformed. Many voters now get their election news in bits and pieces on their Facebook or Twitter newsfeeds, which roll out stories tailored to the individual's interests, friendship networks, likes and dislikes, and political views. Increasingly those bits and pieces appear on users' mobile devices—phones and tablets. Many voters seek out partisan websites that aggregate ideologically compatible stories from a variety of outlets—some respectable, some not. Online, voters might encounter a viral video showing a candidate committing a verbal gaffe or awkwardly interacting with voters. There's a good chance that video will be ridiculed on a late-night comedy program, where many younger voters get much of their news. Older voters might tune in to a talk show on television or on the radio, where their existing views are affirmed rather than challenged.

Yet for all the changes to the media environment, many classic tendencies remain. Donald Trump's campaign for the 2016 Republican nomination was primarily an old-fashioned earned media operation. He made news by leading the polls, beating expectations, and saying outrageous things. Donald Trump was an irresistible story; no wonder he dominated news coverage during the pre-primary stage of the election. Trump was great for television, and television is where many Americans still get their news. Many Americans still get their news "by appointment" rather than "on demand." That is, they watch a news program—live—at a particular time every day, or they read their local newspaper every morning over coffee. The Associated Press and other mainstream news organizations still do most of the reporting that appears not only in newspapers, but also online in the form of websites, blogs, news aggregators, and social media newsfeeds. Talk show hosts still read from the headlines. Candidate scandals and gaffes still get traction primarily through mass media outlets. As a result, candidates are still preoccupied with their news coverage and work hard to shape it. Campaigns still hire press secretaries, grant interviews, hold press conferences, and attempt to "spin" debate performances, poll results, and candidate slip-ups. They still spend hundreds of thousands and sometimes millions of dollars on 30-second spots aired on prime-time television.

This book has catalogued these conventional practices and analyzed their effectiveness. The book also has reviewed new media platforms and sources along with the strategies campaigns employ to reach voters in sometimes innovative ways. Yet campaigns and the media outlets that cover them struggle to keep up with the ever-changing communication environment. So do scholars. Recall the satirical *Onion* headline quoted in the first sentence of this book: "Study: Major Shift in Media Landscape Occurs Every 6 seconds." Exaggeration aside, it is safe to say that major changes are now underway that could alter the candidate/media dynamic yet again. Readers should keep an eye on them. Among the emerging trends and events:

The unrelenting growth of social media for news. Facebook and Twitter show no signs of waning. According to a March 2015 poll conducted by the Pew Research Center, 63 percent of Facebook and Twitter users got news from these two platforms—a significant increase from 2013, when only about half of users turned to Twitter and Facebook for news. Interestingly, the increase occurred among users of all age groups—not just young people (Barthel et al. 2015). As a result, campaigns will continue to broaden their social media outreach, both through paid digital ads as well as "earned" peer-to-peer messaging, surely in more innovative ways than seen in recent elections.

Facebook and Twitter are experimenting with new programs aimed at encouraging news consumption via social media. Facebook recently began allowing media outlets to post stories directly onto its platform rather than on their own sites. That means stories load faster on mobile devices than if they are linked externally to the media outlet's own site. News organizations ranging from *The New York Times* to *BuzzFeed* signed up for the program in its early stages. Twitter recently launched a feature that allows users to follow a live event with a moderator-controlled feed of tweets, images and videos. This sort of feature could transform how debates, conventions and other campaign events are followed by voters and covered by other media outlets. With Twitter, users can watch the event, focus on highlights and monitor reactions through a single platform and device.

Ahead of the 2016 race, Facebook reached out to all of the major presidential aspirants as well as down-ballot candidates. The company pitched several new tools enticing to campaigns, including improved video capabilities and a feature that allows candidates to hold question-and-answer sessions with voters—not unlike Reddit's popular AMA ("ask me anything") function. Facebook also began allowing campaigns to upload their voter files—lists of registered voters along with data for predicting their political behavior—to foster the sort of online microtargeting described in Chapter 5 (Parker 2015).

The continued escalation of independent groups. We can expect to see more independent advertising as super PACs and other outside groups expand their reach. At least on the Republican side, independent groups are raising more money than ever while taking on more of the responsibilities normally handled by the campaigns. Early in the 2016 presidential race for the Republican nomination, independent groups were outraising the candidates' campaigns by a three-to-one margin (Gold and Narayanswamy 2015). All of the major Republican candidates had at least one super PAC devoted to supporting their respective bids. Some of them also benefited from the support of non-profit organizations which, unlike Super PACs, are not required to disclose their donors.

Under federal law, neither super PACs nor non-profits are supposed to coordinate their efforts with the campaigns of the candidates they support—hence the label "independent." But groups are finding increasingly creative ways of getting around the law. Many of them are staffed by former advisers to the candidates—people with first-hand experience with the campaign's broad strategy and messaging, not to mention with the candidate and former co-workers on the staff. Legally, "operatives on both sides can talk to one another directly, as long as they do not discuss candidate strategy" (Gold 2015: A4). During much of the 2016 pre-primary stage, groups and the campaigns were allowed to talk to each other about the ads the groups were running on behalf of the candidate. A Jeb Bush-allied super PAC Right to Rise filmed footage of him for use in the group's ads later on. Such close collaboration has drawn the ire of reformers. "The rules of affiliation are just about as porous as they can be, and it amounts to a joke that there's no coordination between these individual super PACs and the candidates" (Gold 2015: A4).

(Most) traditional media continue to struggle—but online news providers are making strides. Television audiences for both local news and the nightly network news seem to have rebounded, as have their advertising revenues. But on the cable side, audiences have declined for Fox News, CNN and especially MSNBC. Newspaper circulation and advertising revenue continues to decline; in 2014, ad-base revenue was half of what it was ten years earlier (Mitchell 2015). The continued revenue struggles for print is particularly bad news because newspapers still provide most of the basic reporting for news content consumed and shared

online. Digital advertising continues to grow, but it still makes up a small portion of a newspaper's total revenue. Even when a news story goes viral via Facebook or other digital platform, the newspaper that produced it sees only a small portion of the advertising revenue.

The good news is, several online-only news sites appear to be financially viable and are making their own contributions in terms of original reporting and analysis. Politico has expanded beyond its original focus on inside-the-beltway politics to open bureaus in Florida, New Jersey and even Europe. Vice News, launched in 2014, supplies a large number of online video-based reports and full-length interviews in addition to text-based stories. Vox.com, with its emphasis on clearly presented and easily navigable information and analysis, met its revenue goals and exceeded its traffic goals during its first few months of existence in 2014 (Mitchell 2014). These and other online news outlets are partly compensating for the decline in reporting resources elsewhere in the news industry. But these outlets are national in scope—nonfactors for candidates not running for the Presidency. Local television stations have the resources to contribute but, as we saw in Chapter 1, they continue to provide very little reporting on elections.

The departure of Jon Stewart and Stephen Colbert. This final point may seem the least consequential, but perhaps not to many readers of this book. John Stewart hosted his last episode of *The Daily Show* in August 2015. He had hosted the show since 1999. Stephen Colbert aired his final *Colbert Report* in December 2014 after 11 seasons. As we saw in Chapter 2, Stewart and Colbert inspired a great deal of speculation—as well as empirical analysis—on their importance as opinion leaders and information providers. Clearly the Obama White House appreciated Stewart's influence: in 2011 and 2014, the host was invited to meet with the President and his communications team to share notes on policy and young voter outreach (Shear 2015). In one of the final episodes, Obama jokingly issued an executive order preventing Stewart from leaving the show.

Their exits are important because so much of the analysis of political comedy's impact centered on Stewart and Colbert. Through mockery and wit, they gave voice to their viewers' left-leaning political views as well as their exasperation with the politicians and the media who cover them. Can they be replaced? Ratings for their network, Comedy Central, declined by double digits between 2014 and 2015 as it struggled to adapt to young viewers' shift from cable to mobile (Weiner 2015). Stewart passed the baton to South African comedian Trevor Noah, whose introduction was shaken by the revelation that he had once tweeted offensive jokes about women, Jews and Asians. Critics praised *Daily Show* correspondent Larry Wilmore's spin-off show, which moved into Colbert's after-*Daily Show* time slot, but initial ratings fell far short of the show it replaced.

Perhaps the most buzzworthy show has been *Last Week Tonight* hosted by John Oliver, another *Daily Show* veteran. The show's network is HBO, which usually limits viewing to paid subscribers. Yet HBO posts large segments of the program on YouTube, enabling free online access. A number of Oliver's segments have gone viral, sometimes eliciting reactions strong enough to trigger policy change. For example, during the 2014 debate over net neutrality, Oliver urged viewers to voice their objections to the Federal Communication Commission to proposals to roll back existing policy. Oliver's rallying cry brought thousands of visitors to the FCC's website, crashing its servers. Eventually the FCC adopted a pro-neutrality position that was consistent with Oliver's argument. Not surprisingly, speculation has begun about a "John Oliver Effect" (Luckerson 2015).

How will Oliver and other comedians shape current and future elections? Broadly speaking, what is next in the universe of media and elections? Stay tuned.

References

Barthel, Michael, Elisa Shearer, Jeffrey Gottfried, and Amy Mitchell. 2015. "News Use on Facebook and Twitter Is on the Rise." Pew Research Center, July 14. http://www.journalism.org/2015/07/14/the-evolving-role-of-news-on-twitter-and-facebook/.

Gold, Matea. 2015. "Super PACs' Role Grows ever Larger." *The Washington Post*, July 7. A4.

Gold, Matea, and Anu Narayanswamy. 2015. "2016 Fundraising Shows Power Tilting to Groups Backed by Wealthy Elite." *The Washington Post*, July 15. http://www.washingtonpost.com/politics/2016-fundraising-shows-power-tilting-to-groups-backed-by-wealthy-elite/2015/07/15/4c915a74-2b05-11e5-a250-42bd812efc09_story.html?hpid=z1.

Leibovich, Mark. 2015. "Being Hillary." *The New York Times Magazine*, July 19. 32–37, 52, 55.

Luckerson, Victor. 2015. "How the 'John Oliver Effect' is Having a Real-Life Impact." *Time*, Jan. 20. http://time.com/3674807/john-oliver-net-neutrality-civil-forfeiture-miss-america/.

Mitchell, Amy. 2014. "State of the News Media 2014." Pew Research Center, March 26. http://www.journalism.org/2014/03/26/state-of-the-news-media-2014-overview/.

Mitchell, Amy. 2015. "State of the News Media 2015." Pew Research Center, April 29. http://www.journalism.org/2015/04/29/state-of-the-news-media-2015/.

Ornstein, Norm. 2015. "The New York Times' Botched Story on Hillary Clinton." *The Atlantic*, July 28. http://www.theatlantic.com/politics/archive/2015/07/when-the-paper-of-record-fails-to-keep-the-record/399752/?utm_source=SFFB.

Parker, Ashley. 2015. "Facebook Expands in Politics, and Campaigns Find Much to Like." *The New York Times*, July 29. http://www.nytimes.com/2015/07/30/us/politics/facebook-expands-in-politics-and-campaigns-find-much-to-like.html?emc=eta1.

Parker, Ashley, and Nick Corasaniti. 2015. "The Right Baits The Left to Turn Against Clinton." *The New York Times*, May 17: 1, 16.

Shear, Michael D. 2015. "Jon Stewart Met Privately with Obama at White House." *The New York Times*, July 28. http://www.nytimes.com/2015/07/29/us/politics/jon-stewart-secretly-met-with-obama-at-white-house.html.

Weiner, Jonah. 2015. "The Laugh Factory." *The New York Times Magazine*, June 21: 38–45, 52, 55, 57.

INDEX

Taylor & Francis eBooks

Helping you to choose the right eBooks for your Library

Add Routledge titles to your library's digital collection today. Taylor and Francis ebooks contains over 50,000 titles in the Humanities, Social Sciences, Behavioural Sciences, Built Environment and Law.

Choose from a range of subject packages or create your own!

Benefits for you

- » Free MARC records
- » COUNTER-compliant usage statistics
- » Flexible purchase and pricing options
- » All titles DRM-free.

Free Trials Available
We offer free trials to qualifying academic, corporate and government customers.

Benefits for your user

- » Off-site, anytime access via Athens or referring URL
- » Print or copy pages or chapters
- » Full content search
- » Bookmark, highlight and annotate text
- » Access to thousands of pages of quality research at the click of a button.

eCollections – Choose from over 30 subject eCollections, including:

Archaeology	Language Learning
Architecture	Law
Asian Studies	Literature
Business & Management	Media & Communication
Classical Studies	Middle East Studies
Construction	Music
Creative & Media Arts	Philosophy
Criminology & Criminal Justice	Planning
Economics	Politics
Education	Psychology & Mental Health
Energy	Religion
Engineering	Security
English Language & Linguistics	Social Work
Environment & Sustainability	Sociology
Geography	Sport
Health Studies	Theatre & Performance
History	Tourism, Hospitality & Events

For more information, pricing enquiries or to order a free trial, please contact your local sales team:
www.tandfebooks.com/page/sales